ALSO BY MILTON ACORN

DIG UP MY HEART

Milton Acorn

Dig Up My Heart

Selected Poems 1952–83

The Modern Canadian Poets

McCLELLAND AND STEWART

The Canadian Publishers
McClelland and Stewart Limited
25 Hollinger Road, Toronto M4B 3G2

Canadian Cataloguing in Publication Data

Acorn, Milton, 1923–
  Dig up my heart
(The Modern Canadian poets)
Includes index.

ISBN 0–7710–0003–0

I. Title. II. Series.

PS8501.C64A6 1983   c811'.54   c83–094171–1
PR9199.3.A18A6 1983

Grateful acknowledgement is made to the Ontario Arts
Council for its assistance.

Author's photo by: Herbert Lee
Set in Kennerley by The Typeworks, Mayne Island, B.C.
Printed and bound in Canada by T. H. Best Printing Co.

To the just Neruda,
Nobel laureate, spitefully murdered;
and for Jim Deahl, Reshard Gool,
and Hilda Woolnough

plus to the drivers
and staff of City Cabs,
Charlottetown...

CONTENTS

Part One

1952–69

There are more things in heaven and earth, Horatio,
Than are dreamt of in your philosophy.

Shakespeare's *Hamlet*, Act 1, Sc. 5

PASTORAL

That sudden time I heard
the pulse of song in a thrush throat
my windy visions fluttered
like snow-clouds buffeting the moon.

I was born into an ambush
of preachers, propagandists, grafters,
("Fear life and death!" "Hate and pay me!")
and tho I learned to despise them all
my dreams were of rubbish and destruction.

But that song, and the drop-notes
of a brook truckling thru log-breaks and cedars,
I came to on numb clumsy limbs
to find outside the beauty inside me.

A breeze wipes creases off my forehead
and my trees lean into summer,
putting on for dresses,
day-weave,
ray-weave, sap's green nakedness.

Hushtime of the singers;
wing-time, worm-time
for the squab with its crooked neck and purse-wide beak.
(On wave-blown alfalfa, a hawk-shadow's coasting.)

As a sail fills and bounds with its business of wind,
my trees lean into summer.

The glinting long and faintly blue bayonet's a gun's tongue
and drinks sweet wine
though it owns no thirst or malice,
nor do our rockrough millstones of moons and planets
taste the human grain falling, falling
a faint mist of powder
into dark wind. No man's joy
ought to make hate or fate in this game
...there needs to be no losers.

But jokers are tossed in like clubs
ripped green off trees dripping acid,
hilts of weapons arbitrary
with weight and motion stuck into urgent hands
on the do-or-don't spot, balls pitched wary
with malice while the people-pebbled stands cry
"The Umpire! The Umpire! Believe in the Umpire!"

and Dad says, "You'll come to a bad end
if you don't heed the Umpire!"
and Mom says, "I'm sorry, there *is* an Umpire!"
and the Umpire yells
"If your eye gets too gleamy, blink it
or you'll see too bright to look, walk, talk past
the losers! There's got to be losers!"

"In this game there needs to be no losers":
Ike Strange, straight as a runner's thighbone
and arrogant with love, said this
standing at a bank-marble-sharpened corner
while dank air blew men about...
but didn't the wind from his lips
twist me round my pain? and
couldn't that smart buck-toothed accountant
Death, mumble a hardly felt obscenity

and put me down, a few red squigs on the page?
Still I've watched him play, seen him
a secret dreaming on his sharp face
and all his cards turned down, each one
in turn blessed with a touch, a look, a toss
(diamond, spade, fool, hanged man, lover's chariot)
onto the green table.... So long
as he guessed the card his own he'd play it.

In this game there needs to be no losers... I know
the desiccated skins of losers
whisper and rattle past
in every switch of breeze; know
their glue-dim eyes and blasted wishes
tug me to join their flutter: but
in this game there needs to be no losers
tho nearly all lose... I know
my first trump of a yell and heart's jump dealt me in
to muse at my soul's strange faces, and wonder
how chances flow from hand to hand
in this game where there needs to be no losers
and I play my mauled, rainbeaten pack
plus near three billion others, all to win.

My love's got secrets
of dreamplace, sounds
in her ear's core,
keys my fingers
have never played.

Deeds are folded
inside her, some of them
maybe with me.

She's sorting out
our library,
her book, my book,
and now and again
we exchange a touch
for old times.

DEATH POEM

Viki's crying
over a kitten
dead
and the waters
of my brain shake.

God, what is this whisper
of Your existence?

Today the radio blared
news of Marilyn's death.
She, bold with joy
never allowing grief,
left us holding the bag
...a suicide.

I never had to believe
in God, He
believed in me
I've been sure.
Did He believe in Marilyn
and the kitten I buried?

Dead, the atoms lose
intricate jointure,
muscles clot and a
skull once washed with visions
is silent,
milk-stained lips
stiffen.

Viki's tears etch
my insides,
search me

for empty places,
unstick the walls
and open them.
I fear and question
the man I'm becoming.

One violet eye open in a glass stare,
he'd dozed all night in a metal chair,
reminded me so much of you and your old strength
that I bought him coffee for breakfast.

He chuckled around his warmed belly,
this sceptic believing in a strong pulse,
so fierce in his likes, joyous in his hates
he reminded me of you, who
haven't gone hungry for a long time
and find despair a comfort.

Building forms in a mudhole
under the old man's eye,
I said, "Look up!"
at three geese scooting low.

I loved that fusty old
muttering man,
always looking, up, down,
    to the left or
    right of you.

    (He'd scan earth
    at his feet
    as if the house
    stood there,
    him figuring,
    edging,
    adjusting.)
I loved him.

So I bugged him. Told him:
"Listen to the song sparrows,
they've divvied up this property.
We're their people."
or "My balls ring
in tune with this hammer."
I wanted to see his nose
perk and take a good sniff
of the spring air;
    but knew
    sooner or later
    he'd fire me.

Tools, grips sweat-polished,
in a dinted box, loose
at all angles,
half of them vanished.

No gripes today if
old Stan stops too often
to fire up his pipe.

SAINT-HENRI SPRING

Spring I remember wild canaries,
gusts of dandelions
and green tongues of trees
in thoughts of shy ones.

Spring I see a rubber in the gutter,
a broom-handle on a mud lawn;
thaw-water trickles from a pyin udder.

I only see black petals
in the eyes of girls
self-contained as nettles,
choke-cherry sweet in hours
when even the slum grows flowers.

Spring I'm dwelt by startles of canaries,
coronal nudity
stuck to by drab threads of January.

ENCOUNTER

Called from marking
his measured, studied
and guessed sawcut,
the carpenter

rubs back his rusty
forelock, his eyes
groping wide from shiny
cheek-sweat as if

shaken out of a dream
while he tries to fit
his thin (always thin
to him) knowledge

into the bewilderment
of a half-described
blueprint; while
gaining presence

he lets each word,
slant of your chin,
each eyelid flicker
drip from level to level

in his brain
and be counted...
trying to fit you too
into his pictures.

The blue-jays squeal: "More rain! More rain!"
The sky's all blotch and stain.
The colours of Earth are melted down
To dark spruce green and dull grass brown.

Black ducks, last week, held parliament
Up-river there.... Gulls came and went.
Now that they're gone, nor'wester blown,
The grim gulls wheel and bob alone.

Nary a leaf has kept its hold.
The thicket's naked, black and cold.
Then zig-zag, like a skating clown,
The first white flake comes down.

Sunglare and sea pale as tears.
One long hour we watched the black whales
circling like dancers,
sliding dark backs out of water,
waving their heaved tails,
about an eyepupil-round spot
just a knife-edge
this side of the horizon.

OFFSHORE BREEZE

The wind, heavy from the land, irons the surf
to a slosh on silver-damp sand.
The sea's grey and crocheted with ripples;
but shadows, the backs of waves,
lengthen and lapse in the dim haze,
hinting of farther, rougher doings.

The boats went out early, but now
come worm-slow thru haze and distance.
Their gunnels invisible, the men and engines
dots moving on a spit of foam,
they travel past my vision, past
that red jag of a headland, to harbour.

I'd like to mark myself
quiet, like one serene
calligraph in a colour
so subtle it should only
be imagined (something

like a tree in winter
bear its lines and clusters
of snow, as if what's fallen
on it were its own).

I'd like to be quiet
except for a queer grin
that tells nothing but
whatever your own want
takes it as meaning.

But if I'm ever like that
don't believe me. You'll
know that I'm kind of
like a bud...that I'm

waiting for the moment
when I can project
the tip of my tongue
and taste a raindrop

warm.

AN UNTIDY ROOM

An untidy room
is my heart
, because I
can't bear to sweep out
all
of any man

; and the parts left in
are attached by cordy
things that straggle
over the threshold, so I
can't shut the door
tight.

Somebody's retching
down the hall, it
goes on for hours
every day.

Fine background music
for a poem! And then
there's the singing
of the old man
scavenging the garbage;

who used to teach history
so he says. I guess
he was something
besides what he is.

Funny, how time
strips us down
to what maybe
we really are.

One I met in the corridor
had no shoes, only rubbers
flapping on his feet.

As for me I've got no clock
and when I moved in
figured all the alarms
would wake me.

Next morning I overslept.
Everybody here
is on social assistance.

WHY A CARPENTER WEARS HIS WATCH
INSIDE THE WRIST

They say it's guarded better
there, from the bumps of the trade.

I disproved this, and

guessed first those patched people
stuck up like chimneys
in high places, fix them
there so's to look at them
with no long upsetting armswing,
just a turn of the wrist,

but the gruesome truth is
that with the gargoyle-pussed
boss watching, they
don't worry much about balance;

which led me to the real reason
they wear watches tucked close
bouncing and scratching
among all their tools...

it's so they can look quick
out of the lefteyecorner
without the foreman seeing.

Underneath muscles bloodrich and woven
my bones shake
to suddenly know myself beloved
by you, strong and all of a woman.

That word love only tickles
my lip between giggles
until you sing
my name calling me to stand tall
...and that's a swaying thing.

I feel a jolly decorated male bee
about to explode in love's shudder,
like going up in a highspeed elevator
with no floor – only handholds.

But let down your hair, love; let it down
so it hangs low as my navel;
and I'll hold on love, hold on
till we hop all tangled in joy
the whole length of Hell.

REBUTTALS

1

Dear fine-eyebrowed poet
writing of "vengeful owls";
before we use up truth
our tongues'll slough off.
Why waste time telling lies?

2

You with measuring eyes under
lids rumpled like bedclothes;
I know you dote on categories
but why jam me in one?
We've talked just seven seconds.

3

You've slung your truisms like
cases clanking with beer-bottles,
played amateur propagandist and
bayoneted a line of dummies.
Now what do you really think?

4

So... You've damned fools and
reduced time and its stars turning
themselves and space into light
to the compass of an argument?
I don't think everything should stop.

When Joe said, "I'm dying,"
it couldn't damp me,
in his presence
one chuckles for joy.

His truths so innocent,
his lies so innocent,
Joe's innocent,
I'm innocent,
death's innocent.

For the dead
there is no death,
one way or another
not even nothing.

But Joe and those
hearts beating outside mine.
Each one lost crumbles off me,
a piece I've got to regrow.

OF MARTYRS

for Ethel and Julius Rosenberg

I often think of martyrs
and when I do the wind shakes,
and with that pity I can touch their lives,
their flesh,
for they were the most loving of folk.

It was life they chose
not death,
not the staccato small deaths
that leave life a ghost of memories
not really remembered.

They wouldn't lop one verse
from the song of their lives,
wouldn't say the dull fantastic prose
the crazy chants of liars.

Till the last stride with a living instep,
they chose life, not death.

Why man, those hands, dyed
earth and tobacco brown, tough
as an old alligator suitcase, fissured
a dozen extra ways, have
a grip all courtesy, a touch
delicate and sure as a young woman's.

IN MEMORY OF TOMMY, AN ORPHAN,
WHO WAS KIDNAPPED FROM HIS LOVING
FOSTER-MOTHER, KATHERINE, IN FULFILLMENT
OF A BARGAIN BETWEEN CHURCHES

No wonder the boy dreamt of monsters
terrible in horns, mooing his name,
chasing to tickle and eat him; no wonder
these drownpools of eyes looked in
the second-storey window, their bland face
brooding cruel grown-up abstractions;
no wonder that dinosaur with the cooing
dove voice, too big to hide in a barn:
no wonder he woke with terror caught
like a fishbone in his throat, to huddle
amidst a dark full of faces.

I don't know if hate's the armour of love;
what side he joined, or if he joined: but
when he learned to hate those dreams ended.

POEM

My mother goes in slippers
and her weight thumps the floor,
but when I think of her I think of one smile
when she was young

and to me was a goddess of green age
tho now I remember her young
with hair red as a blossom.

I remember the whole room full of that smile
and myself scampering across the edges.

Now she lives on cigarettes and wine,
goes from potted plant to flower,
knowing the time and manner
of each one's tending.

RESTAURANT SCENE

Take Red the waitress
scrawny and guts and things
sticking every which way,
yet along with her bones she hitches
a corona, a halo of herself.

Take her customer, bitch lady-type,
brains compressed to lips' thinness,
yet in Red's aura her talcumed face
relaxes into humanity: her voice
rejoices not far from a chuckle.
Now Red's gone and that mouth's
prepared for cruel words, clamped
by cruel ropes of muscle.

In addition to the fact I lost my job for a nosebleed
In addition to the fact my unemployment insurance stamps
     were just one week short
In addition to the fact I'm standing in line at the Sally Ann for
     a breakfast of one thin baloney sandwich and coffee
In addition to all that it's lousy coffee.

Over drab-shingled peak,
skating on land-buffed air,
white as sun-fierce snow
on a great height,
white
beneath a dirty woollen sky.

His beak, a hooked pencil-mark,
scratches arrogance on brittle gusts.
A refugee from the storm,
it seems his own:
his baleful prophecy.

Hear with the wind still, the grass still,
sharp and erect like animal ears,
its green darkened,
the air and its light dark green,

birds hidden in the just trembling
leaves, chirping hoarse wonder,
and one white butterfly dancing into shade
the rustle of the rain coming on.

LIBERTAD, the sculptor, teaches poetry
to me:
          "Freedom, my freedom
composed of the stone's, the steel's
freedom to find by me its form in
this time, this I and it, this place."

For me it's the tight-grinned nod of
a girl fighting passion as
I recite Spender; and
night and city lights' subdued
shadow of green on clouds and
nighthawks crying, bounding from
curve to taut curve in air; and
throbbing among turbines the
gutted consonantal speech of
a rigger, ex-seaman; the
ring of the struck spike bouncing
hammer and arm into the blows' beat.

And Libertad: his wire-black beard
cropped to let him mask as a welder; or
black-sweatered, all angles
strained into his deed with iron; or
talking, his tensile torso tossed
back into an arm's gesture: he too
is my poetry, my freedom.

An old docker with gutted cheeks,
time arrested in the used-up-knuckled hands
crossed on his lap, sits
in a spell of the glinting water.

He dreams of times in the cider sunlight
when masts stood up like stubble;
but now a gull cries, lights,
flounces its wings ornately, folds them,
and the waves slop among the weed-grown piles.

Past that frost-cracked rock step
twist yourself thru
skewgee trunks and old coat-hook branches;
ground once dug and thought of and
never intended for those toadstools.

In the shade past the crashed robins' nest,
past that spilt sunlight see,
his grainy grip on
a hatchet keened to a leaf,
a man in murky denims
whispering curses to the weeds.

Since I'm Island-born home's as precise
as if a mumbly old carpenter,
shoulder-straps crossed wrong,
laid it out,
refigured to the last three-eighths of shingle.

Nowhere that plough-cut worms
heal themselves in red loam;
spruces squat, skirts in sand;
or the stones of a river rattle its dark
tunnel under the elms,
is there a spot not measured by hands;
no direction I couldn't walk
to the wave-lined edge of home.

In the fanged jaws of the Gulf,
a red tongue.
Indians say a musical God
took up His brush and painted it;
named it, in His own language,
"The Island."

MIKE

You, Mike, twisting on words as if
they flushed your kidneys with daylight,
your sunset's smoggy green, hot orange,
and shunters scoot throbbing thru
muddled smoke and the noises of iron.

I'm geared different, Mike, to a nod
and look over wavy water, my name
pronounced with a rolling tongue,
the sky like sails in need of washing
sometimes, then splotched blue,
the wind familiar to my shoulders.

That's me past your image of me:
and the figure I see wincing
at sirens and jack-hammer clatter
is only my image of you, and
behind it, feeding it, is you
with your grin showing one eyetooth,
reckoning the works of a man, tracing
the routes of wire or politics, exclaiming
at your own sudden understanding.

At El Cortijo, with coffee
tilting right and left
in talk weird as alcohol,
a little dark one backed
into my knee, didn't
look round . . . just sat on it.

No introduction! She took
my femur for a public perch,
and in that exhilarant
fluctuation of conversation
quivered
like a kitten ready to bounce.

I wrung myself with love
for the finely wound nerve of her,
balanced there,
and the way loose hairs
half-twisted
at her palpitating nape.

Disturbed by my rude eye
she twitched round to glare
my grin into a grimace,
then looked back
but didn't budge
her delicate handful of a bum.

After the dim blue rain
swarms of innocent flying things
(green things, curly-bodied things,
things shaped like an arrowhead)
tiny with outsize wings

go wherever the wind wobbles
among pinwheeling swallows
and meet uncomprehended harm
in blond thickets on my forearm.

THE TROUT POND

for R.F. Acorn, 1897–1968

The woods, spruce twisted
into spooky shapes,
echo the trickle of water
from raised oars.

Above the pale ripples
a redwing blackbird fastens,
legs crooked and beak alert,
to a springing reed.

My father's whiteheaded now,
but oars whose tug
used to start my tendons
pull easily these years.

His line curls, his troutfly drops
as if on its own wings,
marks a vee on the mirrored
ragged spruceheads, and
a crane flapping past clouds.

What an elusive target
the brain is! Set up
like a coconut on a flexible stem
it has 101 evasions.
A twisted nod slews a punch
a thin gillette's width
past a brain, or
a rude brush-cut to the chin
tucks one brain safe under another.
Two of these targets are
set up to be knocked down
for twenty-five dollars or a million.

In that TV picture in the parlour
the men, though linked move to move
in a chancy dance,
are abstractions only.
Come to ringside, with two
experts in there! See
each step or blow pivoted,
balanced and sudden as gunfire.
See muscles wriggle, shine
in sweat like windshield rain.

In stinking dancehalls, in
the forums of small towns,
punches are cheaper but
still pieces of death.
For the brain's the target
with its hungers
and code of honour. See
in those stinking little towns,

with long counts, swindling judges,
how fury ends with the last gong.
No matter who's the cheated one
they hug like a girl and man.

It's craft and
the body rhythmic and terrible,
the game of struggle.
We need something of its nature
but not this;
for the brain's the target
and round by round it's whittled
till nothing's left of a man
but a jerky bum, humming
with a gentleness less than human.

CYNICISM

Notice the bums are little guys?
Caps cocked sidewise,
Too big,
Faces brown-grey and wrinkled like a fig.
Funny...all little guys.

Ever stand in a shape-up?
An ape of a pusher puts his finger up,
"Com'ere Joe."
And "Joe" is usually big;
Little men linger against the wall, then go.

Even to look at one's a feast
For your sense of virtue.
"Why not work," you say, "'twont hurt you."
They get less sympathy than wingless flies.
Funny...all little guys.

The child and the old man's eyes
big and wild as a stallion's.
The child I growing, wanting
towards wizardry and competence.

I've dreamt wizards so competent
suns spun side-on to
a nudge from their spare fingertips.

In his brain-pan dreams, the
intricate tension of atoms,
worlds, and him poised
about to dance into them.

Weeks after her abortion,
Clutches of bone
(A thin nearly straight one,
A rib cage, a spine)
Came into the world-light.

Last was the skull and
Pelvis ... which she wore
For a charm.

One day in a lifetime
I saw one with wings
a pipesmoke blur
shaped like half a kiss
and its raspberry-stone
heart winked fast in
a thumbnail of a breast.

In that blink it
was around a briar
and out of sight, but
I caught a flash
of its brain
where flowers swing
udders of sweet cider;
and we pass as thunderclouds or,
dangers like death, earthquake, and war,
ignored because it's no use worrying....

By him I mean. Responsibility
Against the threat of termination
by war or other things
is given us as by a deity.

IMAGES FOR THE SEASON

1

pussy-willows reflected
on ripples, flutter
like bands of butterflies

2

my girl cries look
at a thin-necked robin
strained up, clearing
his throat for a song

3

a foal among
rags of april snow
spring's wobbled up to me
and nudged me
with his milky nose.

ASHAYE DANCING

When Ashaye with the nerve-devouring fire
in her eyes, Ashaye
with her body's secret places,
when Ashaye dances;

The severe dark of her leotards
eats the song in the blood
while her soles slap stark and
the blacks of iron,
of hailstorms,
become her limbs and torso
forms axing, blasting
with her brain all one austere eye
brooding within its motion.

She's blots, destructions
each washing out the last
but revolving into me
so I'll go a host to them
as my thoughts'll walk one day
not as words but steel and marrow.

My breathing's the only music
till she stills, hangs a moment
on a thought, then straightens,
loosens, becomes
Ashaye again, wild-eyed lover
mother and wilful girl.

"CALLUM"

in memory of a novice miner

He had hair like mustard-weed;
shoulders a scoop;
eyes a lake you see the rocks on bottom;
and his voice swung a loop
with music in what it said
that tangled inside your head.

"Callum" was his name
 – pronounced as if he'd sign it on the sun.
From "The Island" he came:
don't know which one.

We dropped to work in our cage,
hearts somewhere behind on a parachute.
That pusher was cute
 – saw him a guy who'd count doing right important,
put him at a hard job beside a well
...a hundred and forty feet,
and he fell.

Look anywhere:
at buildings bumping on clouds,
at spider-grill bridges:
you'll see no plaque or stone for men killed there*:
  but on the late shift
the drill I'm bucking bangs his name in code
..."Callum":
though where "The Island" is I'll never know.

* Gerry Galagher has since made this untrue, in one case.

TWO PLAYERS

One exultant in stroke and guard,
loses himself, tastes alcohol
in the blood of his bitten lips.
The man-pack's howling
of things to be proved, fades and
he's like the driven and returned ball;
living to the limit when
one of the furies of the game.

The other, with his skin dark
as leathern gear, goes into
the game as a high ordeal,
a test like other tests
to prove his people; and
his heart, an eagle in his chest,
buffeting the cage of ribs,
mad to get out.

These two envy one another,
not for prizes but
in a way neither could imagine
unless he loved as well:
and when they battle in the pit
ricocheting off the walls and each other,
you're seeing the game, man,
as it's improvised in instants
by two players juggling
calm and frenzy;
beating at the hurricane
about their hands and brains.

THE IDEA

It's events itch the idea
into existence. The clawing
pixilating world lofts
the mind and its wrangling images
as contrary, gusty, circling
winds toss, flaunt the flags
(splendrous as if living) of
old duchies, unforgotten empires.

Then something palpable as voltage,
maybe a grim preacher, maybe
a wild thin man on a soapbox,
or even a character lugging
a pail and whitewash brush
(whitewash or smear it's all
a point of view) takes charge:
something you want in a way
savage or happy, takes charge:
the idea grows flesh with nerves
to feel the pain of dismemberment.

But its life is death, and life's
going back to the chewing
creation obeying just itself;
so the herded clouds, dream-beasts
in the eyes' pasture, are torn
to fall like tears, like blood.
Then the idea's more like blood,
something in time with running feet,
with typewriter, with heartbeat.

NOVEMBER BEACH

Every step in the noise
of the ocean tumbling from the skyline
to stone frozen rippled sand
is shaken in the shaking wind.

The water of your eye freezes
in one glance outward
to the ducks racing, beaks open,
tagging, zig-zagging
amidst the bullets of spray.

CANADIAN WINTER, 1960–61

Up Spadina, feet like the slow end
of a mutt sniffing from trashcan to pole,
(smutty, scruffy, sour-fat on a thin dole,
pausing whole minutes to lick his behind)
regularly – rain, tea-weak sun, or blinding
snow-glutted poundage of a cold gale –
grey, jawdroopy with ragged lips, the pale
men past forty peg to the breadline.

They've washed in the dirty water of boredom
and in thinly conscious ways are still here;
but predictable in fluctuation
as spasms of malarial fever
or winged ant exodi. My bizarre sir
stop a minute! think of the word "human."

Hungry men, their grins tight with embarrassment,
move by clever steps to intercept me
on the spit-grey downtown streets.
With my wrinkled shoes, my coat ill-used and borrowed,
I wonder how they know me.

One showed me his road-rough palms:
"Look, aren't these worker's hands?"
Oh many have tricks
to trap me – tired of rage and bored with pity,
into the pain of knowledge:
"This is real . . . This is a man!"

My worried arithmetic's blown out of my brain
and I give . . . a nickel, two dimes, a quarter.
Often they want to shake hands,
but I haven't done it yet
. . . Made a partner in Man's indignity
I ask for nothing but a curse.

As from milky vapour, dust of atoms jostling like hornets,
a nebula swigs great swatches of itself into a new sun
raw with light, ravener to its parent mists, messenger
to far astronomers thirsty for the word, the word
that'll unlock them: I've never lost a faith
or wrenched my roots of eyes from the heart . . .
Each doom to joy and torment's nourished
within an old love, becomes a new focus
pulsing radiation, disrupting
the foggy smut of death about it;
while I still step to the blood's rhythm,
the soul's reason in those old stories
of kings and white-hot new stars, wonderful babes
like Jupiter's yowl making that Island cave boom like an organ,
born to laugh a challenge at the old cruel gods.

Surely at least once when a new star burst thru heaven
three old men forsook the stern fantasies
of mummy-clothes they'd wrapped around the world,
and surely they found at least one babe
who held great bear time by its short tail . . . .
For birth by birth the many-coloured creatures of Earth
break ranks and dance apart calling their names and numbers
to reassemble with shoutings and elbow-digs
in formations first seen by the mindseye of a child.

Christmas I became that ho-ho-ho of a saint
to wind on a balky piebald disbelieving burro
along the wisemen's trail thru a desert of grown-up people
like cactus with its growth stalled in tormented poses:
till housed and run around by squirrels I found the boy Sky
with eyes hazel windows into outré dimensions
now looking out on wonder, now looking in
at wonder . . . I came not with gifts but

for a present of the universe made strange, tumbling
with odd fuzzy animals, blue of high heaven
siphoned down to tank up my brain,
for meteors he caught and sent sizzling past my ears:
and for myself made quaint, totemic
like a thick oak come wobbling, walking
grotesquely on its roots over patches of dark and sunlight.

My room's bigger than a coffin
but not so well made.
The couple on my left drink, and
at two a.m. the old man shouts
of going back to Russia.
About five he or his wrung-out wife
puke up their passage money.

The janitor (pay, five a week
plus a one-bed apartment
with furnace in kitchen) has
one laughing babe at home
and two girls, for lack of room,
in the orphanage.
On holidays they appear
with their soul-smashed faces.

Upstairs the Negro girl
answers the phone, sings my name
in a voice like a bad angel's.
Her boyfriends change
every weekend, like the movies.
But my room's cheap, tho
when the wind shifts north
I wear my overcoat
to type this bitter little poem.

Maybe a six-month-old
then, no more,
your eyes dim with fear,
you remember your weak self

Carried as if on the tide
of a nightmare
into that room with white coats
and meaty moons of faces.

A woman with a starched breastplate,
giant hams and shoulders,
splashed you into cold water,
slashed it into your face.

You choked, fought
a screaming tangle,
and she fought,
repressing curses; till

It seemed you saved your life,
were dried, wrapped
in a towel with a washed-out pattern,
and then you slept.

It shivers me to hear you,
an old man with beautiful hands,
saying, "I'm sure
she was trying to drown me."

1

I see a robin on the rain-soaked lawn.
His heart's a swift electric spark
and wee legs drive in packed explosive hops.

Each action's a life-embodied thought;
each thought reflexive, instant with the deed.
Movement distilled, unseen between its poses,
his pin-holed head
listens for worms' dumb secrecy.

2

The trucks drive by towards the hill,
each with its driver's calculating ear
in the engine's multitudinous beat.

In rage, by hard-rubber teeth,
the hill's dragged down, clawed over.
Voice vaults the scale to triumph, then a gearshift
to its hallelujah of the road.

3

There's a bird whose name I've never heard
only the variations of its song.
It comes between false dawn and dawn
to a black tree and sings to me.

I'll seep down into earth, rise and become that bird:
tune and rhythm tight in tiny brain
to spout thru tonal throat,
ring stratospheric layers with my joy.

Brain liver and whole insides
at a slow burn...
see the smoke in her eyes!

Like hammers rata-tata-tating
at sheet-metal, cold
rain's batting
the night road, the signpost
and she with rivulets in her hair,
hesitating, a reticule
cluttering small souvenirs
in one chill-fixed handhold.

"Go on! travel!" the whip-tongues
of rain speak.... Rips of lightning
for hundredths of seconds
photograph place-names on the sign
like far bird voices, guesses
at exotic works and caresses.

A clapper clanging her bell of a body,
words harshly glad
with tonal sense strange, dialect-ravelled
mad as the rain
hiss.... "Go on! travel!"
But in that darkness blotted with shapes
she must invent her destination,
while each time thunder tumbles
around her earlobes
the letters on the signboard jumble.

After hunger
two days long,
sitting happy before
a plate of beans,

I delicately slit
each kernel with
my incisors,

let my tongue run
twitching with joy
across the texture
of the meat.

As the orange-
striped cat
hunches,
glaring down,

the pale-fluffed
nestlings
he's discovered
feel cooled
in the shadow,

and

stretch their thin
necks, heavy
heads up,
hungry
beaks open,

wide
on hinges.

What maddens me? Listen:
there was greyeyes
eleven-twelve, tall
bony and strong-rumped,
with her little sister browneyes
(their clothes brown
poverty-brown with
straight-banged mother-haircuts).
It was browneyes' birthday
and greyeyes took her
out on the street
to ask a present
from strangers.

Hold on, browneyed poet!
It was likely
a story, but a good one;
and browneyes could hardly speak
with wanting. Needed coaching
from greyeyes, strong
desprit but in command
and in a grim way warm
like a U-boat captain
or Ruski Christ harrowing
Hell in a 57-ton tank.
A good dimesworth story!

What maddens me is
greyeyes' future, always
strong, a little bitter but
not letting it spoil the fun
or her love, strong, decisive.
One night deliberately
leaving her pants home;

and then the ordinary story
of a man with job-wounded hands,
tired, tender
only in bed, or
on the sweet end of Sunday.

Ordinary ... Yet
I rave and like a Samson
poke at the keystone of the world
in desperate hope
that greyeyes' life
won't be at all
ordinary.

Knowing I live in a dark age before history,
I watch my wallet and
am less struck by gunfights in the avenues
than by the newsie with his dirty pink chapped face
calling a shabby poet back for his change.

The crows mobbing the blinking, sun-stupid owl;
wolves eating a hamstrung calf hindend first,
keeping their meat alive and fresh...these
are marks of foresight, beginnings of wit:
but Jesus wearing thorns and sunstroke
beating his life and death into words
to break the rods and blunt the axes of Rome:
this and like things followed.

Knowing that in this advertising rainbow
I live like a trapeze artist with a headache,
my poems are no aspirins...they show
pale bayonets of grass waving thin on dunes;
the paralytic and his lyric secrets;
my friend Al, union builder and cynic,
hesitating to believe his own delicate poems
lest he believe in something better than himself:
and history, which is yet to begin,
will exceed this, exalt this
as a poem erases and rewrites its poet.

YOU GROWING

You growing and your thought threading
the delicate strength of your focus,
out of a clamour of voices,
demanding faces and noises,
apart from me but vivid
as when I kissed you and chuckled:

Wherever you are be fearless;
and wherever I am I hope to know
you're moving vivid beyond me,
so I grow by the strength
of you fighting for your self, many selves,
        your life, many lives... your people.

JANUARY SPARROW

Two rusty wires jammed rubbing
make music in January. Look up
and on a wire between two snow-tufts
a grey puff of a sparrow's
fluffed warm in this dank wind.

January Armstrong
make the air cringe again
with a song come via your gearbox larynx
from a heart big as a diesel engine!

A creation, but once the substance
was given pattern, painted
the colours of night, manbone and blood,
sculpted into men with sure powers,
it acquired its own laws, moves
and their effects having nothing
to do with its creator's tinted vision.

Yet the tool, the vision's needed
in the mindseye of the player, the
reflection of squares and mock men
moving, building the concept which
must have truth and its own growth
or be shattered on the cruel board.

What's fatal isn't the vision but
confusion of vision with the hard board,
the feel of godhead manipulating
men according to exact fancy, to
miss or with fine passion deny
the relentless laws, the powers of men.

REQUEST

Be young... Walk impudently humming
– hair a lemon cloud inlaid with sunset,
between ridges of my brain.

I'm all torn murk and lightning
– stink with blood of crocodiles I've wounded.
Be young... Have eyes a sun-leached sky
where swallows whiz in parabolas.

Let a shy hand find your woman hair,
the wee mouth at your breast
be like your chuckle in the bell of my skull
– young, possessed.

It turned out the mattress the landlord'd promised me
was on another couple's bed. Furthermore
it was that bearded man himself who greeted me
and helped me carry it down. They hadn't
paid their rent and I had, so I slept well.

I'd gotten so used to the philosophical conclusion
that everything I had was taken from somebody else
that it didn't bother me at all to be faced with it
concretely; but still here, writing my poems
about the ultimate man, rising like a phallus
to every call for a response – emotional and brave
as all hell . . . I wonder if there's something about being human
    I'm not getting at.

Here's to the bottle I'm drinking
And here's to all the bottles I've drunk;
Rent a quarter-acre for my gravesite
And make a pyramid out of bottles,
Labels out....

Here's to my drinking companions
Even when I've drunk alone...
Rent an acre for my gravesite
And pile us all, soak us in alcohol
And make a special match,
A special engraved souvenir match
To strike a light.

TO A COCKROACH

Itsel ting, thee gives me a big wish
for words in some wee chir-
ped language

Since in the shaaaaaaa-
dow of Earnie's foot, thee stopped
and thy feelers all flit-flutter
went swiftily

not as if thee heared the high distractions
we bowled back and between us;
no – test-tastily thee
widdled the air, an so so so so

sharp thy wittle concern-things
touch-trembled thee ... I see
how thee's got Earnie (old
bullet-in-the-brain-him Earnie) who

thee so pestify
all so absurdily tilted with love.

Thinking of a dove I have never seen
– tobacco leaf feathers, incense smoke and cream,
Eyes that bob black walking, in startled take-off;
Circles those eyes describe in the flutter roar, whisper and
    whistle
Of wings – shadows and shadow colours of thought and the
    world:

That there is no mourning in the dove, nor in its cry
Except in the thought of it there's the thought of tears
Tiny and plump, as things living, running down shadowed face
    flesh;
And in tears, especially quiet ones, all things take beauty's
    texture...

I've cursed death as the realest face of God
– black finger swallowing the buttercup, shadow deeper
Than all the underness of waves; in the tap of that finger
    ...vanishment.
The priest in black and gold of all his robed belly
Threatened death as all the pain-grey flashes
Of the worst of life, as life continuous –
A scream in which the throat's continually torn, fragmented
    and reborn –

But when I was thirteen Confucius appeared in a quotation
And dream as two merry eyes over a beard like sun and moon
    over the woodsy world;
Saying: – "Not know life...How know death?" And silent

As a foetal smile his laugh has grown in what you might call
    my soul.
I've thought of death as an ambiguous flavour, the swiftest
    taste
Which dissolves as you wonder what it's like –
As light fleeing from the last star on the edge of the universe
Its curving wave-front as wings, no eyes behind,
No brother-light or thought of light in front, no thought;
As the tongue-lick of a purring lioness . . . .

And conversely I've denied with less fear than I've denied
My oh-so-bragging, oh-so-punishing Lord, that death's ever
    more real
Than now when my atoms are showering about me
    popping like raindrops
 – that my headstone exists, that any particular moment exists
Sitting like that stone atop my twin gems, serpent eyes
On the head of my patterned trail through time; that anything
    true now
Will still be true on any day in which I will not die.

And yet again I've thought, "I will die . . . "
No fear . . . . The priest's threat was life, not death;
Survival of only part of me, my pain, survival of myself as pain
Only, and every part of me become pain, life
Screaming my wounded name forever and ever
As he had already made me scream it:
This is what I feared, and it's gone
Except in my negating laugh, a little gold flower
Plucked and falling over and over in light wind ripples . . . .

In these days before any of Time's old unthought evils
Dies, it incarnates itself
In a human body, in a brain and spit-slurring tongue
To scheme and argue its eternity:
That there are evil men; that they are evil
May hurt the mind with its truth, but

I predict their deaths, not mine:
And this thought is my comfort –

No fear....But like a little patch of violet
On a calling dove's throat (some imaginary species)
Mourning....I've wept for myself
As a laughing child, like the son I've lost, all the lost
    children –
Pronouncing their names as they're pronounced on my home
    island:
Out of the mouth as out of a bell;
And the waves of a south blue sea have lapped the roots of
    my lashes
As if they were forested shores

If all lights fell on me differently,
If the music differed, and the voices
Were others, perhaps I'd know better
Who I am: but now I can only guess it

Thru my refusals (like some one kind of person
Wonderful maybe, at least strange
Were going through something like an orchard,
Picking up and throwing down). So many things

Of which I say, "Yes...I admire that!"
But what is it keeps me from folding
The whole damn basketful of stars
Into my bosom? Why can't I give

My most personal love, which I've often said
Was universal, whenever it's asked? You need
Such a precise almighty balance with me
As to what you come on with, and what you hold back.

Bright moon. Oh if I could live like my spaniel
To whom all things are urgent and simple,
If not simple, nowhere: If my nerves drank my desires
As hers do... Maybe I could stick up one mysterious finger
And sign the moon as an artist might.

Description isn't for poets. Poetry demands an exactitude
That defies description. Liken the soul to an electron
, but when you say "like" that implies "not quite";
or drop that word: but then you're speaking of something else
        entirely
going on in the nucleus.

Like yesterday I told a man I loved him... And the delight,
The entire going with the necessity of my statement,
Made me ride the next hour like on a surfboard. Poor guy
: he disappointed me. But then... Why be disappointed?

You can smile at a Chinese like that. I've noticed that.
Sort of to say, "You're there... I'm here too... And
Isn't this a crusty cinder we walk on?" Dandelions I love
Because they grow where nobody wants them but the
        children,
The poets, and of course themselves.

"The moon is *not* a paper lantern," I told Roy,
"The moon's a big, jagged, dusty hunk of rock!"
He said, "It is to me." "Okay," I said, "make it a paper lantern
For me!" Which is a lie. It didn't go quite like that:
But similarly I liken the soul to an electron. Give it a charge
And it jumps to a new orbit. Therefore I praise the jump
Before it happens: Which makes the kids say I tell lies.
Well so I do.... But my lies make things happen.

Against the pink-brown fence with the sprucelet
My little sister stands to be photographed;
Fire tinges from her head and the dandelions –
Tear down the pink-brown fence to make a raft

Tear down the pink-brown fence to make a raft
Where my little sister stands to be photographed
Fish poke up their noses to make rings
And memories of dandelions dance from the ripples....

The camera is too slow to catch the gold
Of dandelions remembered around my little sister;
Stand up the old raft for a painting board
And guess the why of it – you can't recall kissing her....

Cut up the rotten painting for a bonfire;
The flames rush up a rattle, faint boom, and whisper;
Sparks fly gold in the night and then white;
Dandelions, and the hair of my little sister

"Gerry! Gerry!" calls one tramp
to another. The chin
(flushed and dirty) beckons
peremptory as the voice
is meant to be; but the eyes

(are they black, suffused
as it were with the dust of pavements
, who can tell?) they plead,
and for that matter so does the voice

: for it's a matter of doubt if
Gerry will answer. Sure you
can take it for granted they've wet the mouth
of the same bottle (the man's call
with its garbagecan echoes, tells you that) n
number of times; but picture

what a bending down from an
unforgotten hope of dignity
any touch is down here, let alone
an acknowledgement of the things shared

implied in that call, desperate in its way
as the smallest things have come to be desperate
in my world as well as theirs.

I'll cast a silver bullet and bless it with my holiest kiss,
fire it just once and it'll rise
singing like a lark. Now and then it'll dive
down and delightedly thru the heart of one of those I hate.

Oh the "chirp-chirp-chirp" of its passing! Infants'll look up
and their eyes become drops of quicksilver at the thought that
        the world at last has a guardian
: and I, long since dead, will be at peace except in one of those
        moments
when it plunges and one more whorl of evil winks out

... then the watchers of my skeleton
will notice that for a moment my skull's grin
is a little broader.

At that instant I heard the scream of this bubble of a universe
Or bubble on the universe in a conflagration of dimensions
– It's all the roaring ages' long scream of expansion –

An artist in shorts squatted above me in a cage hung from the
    ceiling
Playing a board, stabbing the light with flashes of dark, the
    dark with injections of white fury
As his mates did, and other things – for what they had
    bandied and rolled about among their own yelling brains
Was not *what* I *should* see but that I should see some *thing*:

Between us the sparkle-eyed nervy unaged machine, alum-grey
    and like a clean page of fluctuating nothing,
Snatched away the sky like a sheet or a tablecloth
And the two worlds of Heaven and Earth tumbled and
    mixed . . .

LIVE WITH ME ON EARTH UNDER THE
INVISIBLE DAYLIGHT MOON

Live with me on Earth among red berriés and the bluebirds
And leafy young twigs whispering
Within such little spaces, between such floors of green, such
      figures in the clouds
That two of us could fill our lives with delicate wanting:

Where stars past the spruce copse mingle with fireflies
Or the dayscape flings a thousand tones of light back at the
      sun –
Be any one of the colours of an Earth lover;
Walk with me and sometimes cover your shadow with mine.

The twist, the bend or arching up
to kiss, always includes – with me
, a watching of myself. It's a stepping
into strangeness, becoming the man
of hoped-for truth, who moves in the blood.

Was it so with Judas? The step towards
the man moving in grace, the clutch
and the shape his body took, lips leading
... was it felt? Was the betrayal
felt as if two men, the mover and the motion
were there, balanced in the walk and the stop?

It's a ceasing to be the dry grainy self
of affairs, the bringing of another
into the arms' loop, the compass
the body contains for itself. Like
receiving a kiss, it's the new breath
of a new spirit, allowed by yours
in the presence you carry ... and a living guess
included in your memories, hopes and urges.

A new complexion of colours. The god (the thing
out there that's the tone of kindness) comes down
for you both, into you both. Two people stand
for a wonderful one, as if it were a new person.

I'm thinking of a sudden kiss I got from
a stranger I'd been watching, and thus knew
she'd been watching me ... in a crazy coffee house
where she used to come and go dancing
from table to table, kissing all

she acknowledged part of the company
... a contract to love and be loved.

Thus it'll be when the last rabbi crowns
the Messiah.... It'll be a kiss
he's topped with, and all enraptured souls
will kiss and joyfully allow each other to exist.

DETAIL OF A CITYSCAPE

Have you noticed
how the cripple
struggles
onto the bus?

From where I sit
a hand,
white-knuckled
on the rail
is all I see;

and then the parts,
a head, an aimless
cane flopping,
hooked to a wrist,
levering elbows,
the poor twist
of a torso,
finally those disobedient
feet.

Once on, he lurches
onto the unrailed bench
next to the driver
... the most uncomfortable seat;

because if he tried for another
the surge of the bus starting
would upend him.

In the uncurling light, relentless it is
hurting towards the roots of my passion
day by day my beauties fall into me

each wanting me a pool for a freedom. Oh the sun's my
    reflected eye
and I walk one upright finger tickling my bluesky God.
The children are pennies, bright
as my giving glance and though the cars run on my loneliness
oneday soon I'll stop them all and shake hands with each
    driver.

Birds are my newsboys, calling
the minutes of the just who loft their heads among them,
and the worms are tailors sewing my suit with themselves for
    threads.
A rose stands forever bursting and still, pink
as the inside of my eyelid, and I'm stopped unwavering
on the wavering road, living on the inward parts of a moment.

"Since there's no God ... everything is forbidden,"
read the mottoes on the billboards. I know
the enforcers are armed, that it's a miracle I exist, that it's a
    miracle
I continue to be a miracle. Because I've defied them
a day opens ten thousand wings. As long as I've got one
    sound tooth
I'll gnaw this greenearth biscuit. No my dear demanding sirs
I will *not* turn a triple somersault thru my asshole.

The king rains like a bloody waterspout
that gathers in the elements and spews them out
onto the noses pointing him, the upturned
pack of eyes, the brocade of the courtly city.

Truly he rains. Ask the sad hounds, worshippers
in the loaded wind, how all men rain, how every draught
bears fragments escaped from their urgencies.
Maybe this is why the dogs know better....

By no reflections, by no estranged energies
bouncing in their own crazy context, do they know
their gods, or for that matter their devils, but
by particles just shook loose... homunculi perhaps.

The king eats, and the lowly vegetable, the stupid
moo-cow flesh becomes royalty – grand gestures, surges
of vision inpainted with power... And out
it goes! Ah manure! That once tottered so high!

Gurgled from the sewers of history, the rivers bear it
to plebian seas. The clerk, paid less than a labourer,
tidies his balls' threadbare covering and still votes
conservative. Does that dirty worn string, the continuum
of his consciousness, still wave in fantastic breezes?

The king points down his beard and listens. Oh grandly
does he permit the light whose flux is the blood of souls
to illuminate even his royal planet of a heart! "I am
your friend... oh let my worshipful word clothe itself
in your proud and glorious body!" And the king says,
"Friend! What does it mean? What interest of mine
can you fulfil? Which do we have in common?" "Inwardness,

outwardness . . . And the going to and fro between them,"
the councillor, if he were wise and brave, might answer

if the king were not a fool. Then he might look up
and see himself take shape in the king's eyes,
as if we all bore shields like mirrors, and the reflection
made the object, or else our meanings
dropped sizzling into the crucibles of one another's wills.

The king's a secret heretic. "Look at my hunting pack,"
he thinks. "How well they know what men are! And what
        makes men?
My pleasure! How wrong
it is to say that I've got no dominion over souls!"

The king tells his confessor, is forgiven, feels a chilled moment
the winds of imagination blowing through him; peasants
sowing his bones; armourers hammering out his shape.
Last night he dreamt he was a splattering pool

and his rain was a rain of bloody sweat. Splashes made rings
that ran out crisscrossing to his farthest edges. Then suddenly
some clouds – some men – would no longer rain, but stood
        over him
: shadowing. He woke up crying, "Revolution!"

He slept again and dreamt he was a spark
hissing along the fuse of time.

POEM

Hair flowing yellow and still
to her shoulders, I
saw my sister once
stand before a new flower
and in a hushed voice
give it a name:

and as she cupped
her first gardenia
under her collarbone
today I held
as a vein round my heart
an unwritten poem;

a word – a few words
delicate as linked blossoms,
more delicate
being thoughts, and
only when winds start
licking them to nothing

do I write so
I may bring you my poem
to find the music of a name,
its vowel-tones to my ears
as a flower reflected in her eyes.

In winter twilight on a side street,
black – touched at the edges by snow,
with secondhand cars parked headlight to trunk,
a deadeye glow in each window,
I heard a "clip-clop," "clip-clop"
ringing as if the earth was hollow.

And all white with his tall ears
dusting the underside of heaven, a Clydesdale
with mighty brushes of hair on his hooves
swelled and swept from the shadows
... One moment I stood in his friendly eye
then like a lord he passed me.

With all the pride of his vanished race
he switched his big wind of a tail,
then turned a corner
and his hoofbeats abruptly stilled,
leaving one steaming brown bun
and a hush as if sparrows were listening.

Always you become more real
Without ever being really;
The eternal approach
With never a touching –

You are like the light on my table
Forever changing hairdos, hats and shades;
So whatever shape is kindly or malignant
I must judge in your spray of tints....

So I thought, and so I think
When all of which I say "are"
Has become "were" – you stink
In my memory, dark bee-catching flower;

Devourer of the pretty, spitter-out
Of men's just remnants like seeds;
I'm thinking of a light drizzle in the sun
Fallen through poison....

I've gone and stained with the colour of love
The two-hundred-and-fifty-pound road foreman
Gone on his liquor, who sits
On my wicker armchair and strains it
So much in every binding point it can't even creak.

I've known him as a laugh-cursing soldier;
I've known him posed decisively as a statue
Out on the road, telling them what to do.
I've known him so much sufficing himself
Carrying his lunchpail....
                              But here he sits
And his eyes are like a bull's except
A bull's eyes don't hurt and his do....

Or does a bull cast such a poignant hurtful look
At the slaughterer between the blow and his collapse?
I've gone and stained with the colour of love
Bulls too; and this man is called Bull...
He says to me, "Milt – You old bastard!"
And I say, "Bull – You old bastard!"
We've told each other about all our nicknames:
But his life was this – His Childhood and The War;
And all that followed was a disappointment

I've gone and stained with the colour of love
Life: – Well here is a man who knows life....
We tell each other about our wives
His dead, mine lost, his lost before her death:
And I say, "Bull, you old bastard!"
And he says, "Milt, you old bastard!"

It being the admission of manhood
That each has done wicked things.
So we pitch arguments back and forth;
But sometimes he just sits and watches me work.

Wisdom makes us hesitant
. . . true, but
it's no wisdom that doesn't sometimes
make us bold

; or wish to be bold. No one wise
as I hope
          I am
                    could look
into the dewy country of
your smile
and not think of loving.

There are few things left for
a heart echoing like mine is
. . .the horses are gone
        , the sparrows
are rare: in this far land the robins
sound embarrassed

                    . . .

      but I love the way you sing,
    almost whispering, as if you thought aloud
among the ridges
                    of each man's or woman's
ear.

In the elephant's five-pound brain
The whole world's both table and shithouse
Where he wanders seeking viandes, exchanging great farts
For compliments. The rumble of his belly
Is like the contortions of a crumpling planetary system.
Long has he roved, his tongue longing to press the juices
From the ultimate berry, large as
But tenderer and sweeter than a watermelon;
And he leaves such signs in his wake that pygmies have fallen
And drowned in his great fragrant marshes of turds.

In the elephant's five-pound brain
The wind is diverted by the draughts of his breath,
Rivers are sweet gulps, and the ocean
After a certain distance is too deep for wading.
The earth is trivial, it has the shakes
And must be severely tested, else
It'll crumble into unsteppable clumps and scatter off
Leaving the great beast bellowing among the stars.

In the elephant's five-pound brain
Dwarves have an incredible vicious sincerity,
A persistent will to undo things. The beast cannot grasp
The convolutions of destruction, always his mind
Turns to other things – the vastness of green
And of frangibility of forest. If only once he could descend
To trivialities he'd sweep the whole earth clean of his tormentors
In one sneeze so mighty as to be observed from Mars.

In the elephant's five-pound brain
Sun and moon are the pieces in a delightfully complex ballgame
That have to do with him... never does he doubt
The sky has opened and rain and thunder descend
For his special ministration. He dreams of mastodons

And mammoths and still his pride beats
Like the heart of the world, he knows he could reach
To the end of space if he stood still and imagined the effort.

In the elephant's five-pound brain
Poems are composed as a silent substitute for laughter,
His thoughts while resting in the shade
Are long and solemn as novels and he knows his companions
By names differing for each quality of morning.
Noon and evening are ruminated on and each overlaid
With the taste of night. He loves his horny perambulating hide
As other tribes love their houses, and remembers
He's left flakes of skin and his smell
As a sign and permanent stamp on wherever he has been.

In the elephant's five-pound brain
The entire Oxford dictionary'ld be too small
To contain all the concepts which after all are too weighty
Each individually ever to be mentioned;
Thus of course the beast has no language
Only an eternal pondering hesitation.

In the elephant's five-pound brain
The pliable trunk's a continuous diversion
That in his great innocence he never thinks of as perverse,
The pieces of the world are handled with such a thrilling
Tenderness that all his hours
Are consummated and exhausted with love.
Not slow to mate every female bull and baby
Is blessed with a gesture grandly gracious and felt lovely
Down to the sensitive great elephant toenails.

And when his more urgent pricking member
Stabs him on its horrifying season he becomes
A blundering mass of bewilderment . . . . No thought
But twenty tons of lust he fishes madly for whales
And spiders for copulation. Sperm falls in great gouts

And the whole forest is sticky, colonies of ants
Are nourished for generations on dried elephant semen.

In the elephant's five-pound brain
Death is accorded no belief and old friends
Are continually expected, patience
Is longer than the lives of glaciers and the centuries
Are rattled like toy drums. A life is planned
Like a brushstroke on the canvas of eternity,
And the beginning of a damnation is handled
With great thought as to its middle and its end.

A ragged curtain
And a plant in the window
Of the little house squashed hard
Against the sidewalk.

The house is gone,
Door step crazy,
Boards chewed by weather.
For a while there was a hole
And then it closed
Like an eye winking
And leaving no trace.

Once I knocked on the door
And someone answered who knew me,
Said, "Hello Milton!"
And how he said it was a surprise
Curse blunted by kindness.

The house is gone –
Let's hope they have a better one
For it stands in my thoughts with four corners
As we ought to print a period □

Which is the sun and which is the wind
Sweeping like a yellow broom?
The shadow of my garage – called a studio
By my mother, who must confer me dignity
Creeps with its gable like a spearpoint....

And now its point is lost it tosses
A whole head of shadow-plumes
Borrowed from another tree;
Softened before it reaches the apple-tree –

Where the wind waves leaf-fans
Covering one red apple-face
To open another.... Red balls
Ready to bounce into the mouths of children;
Or maybe if I'm not too lazy
Into applesauce, made by my mother:
The stove is waiting and humming: –

Go little eyes and get yourselves a proper view
By being birds in it – Spill a sky from your throats
With the clouds' balloons for "Gosh" "Wow" "Yeah"

Go the grassflower scented breezes, go my eyes
Set upon ants' heads, prows of fishing canoes, swinging
From charm bracelets, berry-tasting snakes' tongues –

Slide down heaven-in-a-looking-glass to star-grains-of-sugar;
Colour your snow seven ways to fly
Onto my canvas and paint me hilly: –
Come you take me in like a wasp in amber
Fitted onto baby penises, jumping wallaby toes
 – to tickle the wind a willow away....

WORDS SAID SITTING
ON A ROCK SITTING ON A SAINT

IN MEMORIAM: *Red Lane*

I

He had a way of stopping the light
, making it mark his darkness,
and a depth like a sounding line
played out, swinging its futile
weight far above bottom
, drank all his surfaces.

WARNING... Don't tempt the gods
with too much patience, for he poked
for poems as in the sand for stones
 – round firm things, with no entrances

: and would wait for the end
of the time he was in, for
that discovery, the moment of vision
that for him was hard, like a stone

: and I reached out tendrils of thought
towards him.... If he told me what a flower
was to him, I'd tell him what a flower
was to me. Thus we worked on each other,
patiently, as if each was immortal.

His dying is like an infinite grey sphere
of nothingness to the left hand of my sun,
and sometimes I draw the nothingness down
to wrap about me, like a cloak with hood.

The saint of stone silences
is dead. The miracle is
that he does not speak,
even as when he made his sparing
moves in our game, his speakings
were flint fragments of no language,
harder silences.

The miracle is that the Earth still traces
all the circles of her whirling dance,
and those yo-yos of the sun, the comets
still comb their white curly hair
across the heavens, while he
as in life consents to all their courses.

Doomed to his time, he accepted it
and made a gnomic utterance of it. Caught on it
across, like a bow on a fiddle string
he drew the one note it was meant to say
by his agency, and concluded it
with quietness that was its continuation.

I've got quite a face, thank God
for smiling or scowling;
tho the smile doesn't earn me much
(so knowingly innocent

and forgiving of all
they bewilderingly find themselves to be
people wonder what they've done
and edge away from me)

: but the scowl – that's different!
especially when I stick a cigar in it.
If they have any plans
for bringing me crashing down on it

They give them up. Either way
no one believes in the puddle of mother's milk
that almost floats my heart, or how
the miracle of a human being's existence

disarms me. I guess I see enough evil
as it is, without it being tossed like acid
into my eyes
– the way most people get it.

Heartswell in the mind, presence of purple
... to dream of swallowing a colour,
warm ice cream and peace under the navel.

My arts are the impossible shades
I see under closed eyelids, the attributes
with which I caress my friends, not the amendments
time makes as it passes, but the stillness
sudden and lasting of a brainrooted flower.

It's hardest to reconcile oneself to freedom
... the pain of choice, the pain
of another's choice of not you as you want yourself
but part of her own existence;
flowers are quieter; they rest
within your skull as a delicate carved bowl

: and are a tremble, a trickle, a voiceless
kindness that includes a deep light of you, a
loving consent to your life,
                                        a refuge from rage.

O in what power
and tenderness, whatever power
and tenderness you come
to her first time

(having come to terms with the frost
annually, having come to terms
and worked in its lands, having
gone down in the gully where the oriole tries
his voice, and added notes)

(having come on, come on, and
let it come, let it come
having not watered
the nettle of pride, having
touched, retreated and stood a half-step back
a patience of times, and finally
melted into her melting
coming on)

, the time that's in her own terms, you having dared
to guess a swerve into her fall thru free space, O
every rose opens on its own morning, and the sun
the sun.... It's his first too.

ONE DAY KENNEDY DIED
AND SO DID THE BIRDMAN OF ALCATRAZ

(Why was Kennedy killed?
He was a rich war-maker
who was beginning to learn
that war didn't pay –
That no people who resisted
him was helpless....
                        On
the day he died, murdered
no one will admit knowing
by whom –
                Another man
who had done far more good
to the human race,
                        died;
I wrote this poem –

The world rolls,
lives flick off,
rain in the dark.
Oftener than I blink
they fall
, each one more
momentous
than a sun going out.
Shall I make fractions
of my tears? ration to each
one molecule of salt?
How many shots in Texas?
How many hungers
fade only
as the mind fades?

Yet I love Prince Charley
because he's a boy I know of
and a boy's portion is love.
Churchill's cigar, Khrushchev's shoe
are talismans I touch
vaguely with the spirit.
Unlike some friends I don't snarl
"Good riddance!" but
for each one lost I have
a particular kind of sorrow.

For Kennedy, the image-man,
his very soul wired
and tugged into shape
by advertisers, his words
so evidently sincere
and false, false, I mourn
with Sartre
for the hell that is other people
... the man who never was:

But for Stroud in his cell
with a roaring toilet
who just the same fashioned
a heaven of birdsongs
for himself and others,
I cry sincerely
precisely because
the assassin failed

Thinking of Looey and his gestures elegant
like a chess-player (that swallow swoop
of the hand in slow motion, the piece
hooked between thumb and two fingers
, the shorter hop, and the base tilted
an instant on the square, before setting down).

I go on to how the pieces come into our game
telling of themselves in whispery thoughts
while the voices shout, and our hopeful passions
shout, "This is it . . . it!" "Yes or no!"

And Looey, who has so desperately thought
is a failure – his moves all wrong: and
perhaps I, sitting here like a pudgy
statue of "The Thinker," perhaps I
who so earnestly try to explain
what I am and am not . . . ?

Funny . . . I can't think of you as a piece.
My game – if it is a game – 's become inscrutable
and I think only of yours, just begun and
wonder what wonderment you've made of me.

See the chessman in the player's hand, looking up thrilled
, made all one drum of a pulse by the touch: saying
"I love you!" and rejoicing in the words
tho they may go all unheard. How he longs
for the melding of power and concept, that move
which'll make him transcendent!

Each of us both piece and player . . . I sign myself
with your kiss on the inside of my backbone, all given

124

to love which is all of eyes fixed thoughtful on us.
Oh there's Looey, and so many to help... so many games
all to be won: but this is our game, part of them all
, and we are given each other's.

Dear old God, I'm not at odds with Thee;
I've got stronger friends
And more ferocious enemies –

If there's no God there's no atheist god either;
Nothing commands me to acts of villainy,
Nothing commands me to hate what doesn't exist....
And is there a rule against loving It?

PERFECT

Moments of inlet vision, moments
when the ugly world strikes
like a swung door.
All of a sudden . . . .

Perfect! I blew a
smoke-ring. Never
when I try it; but
as for my life it seems a
succession of efforts
. . . gestures really

: then in the act of what's loosely called
"loving" a wave (I swear
all the cells jerk)
washes clean thru me: ·
or I bang my fingertip
down on the page,
"That's IT!" and take off
on rockets
in all directions

. Later I wonder
what did it? Is it the coming
together of me and a symbol
that momentarily becomes
me? a crossing of two
lines always changing
in time? or

a slit of light,
blinding, sudden, and
just for an instant
in the black bag
of another's existence

(her reflexes, her
expediences, her fumbling
love and approximations of living,
even her lies
held to with a desperation
maybe forgotten)?

Whatever it is, it's less
and more than the ideal,
which maybe is just me
and also a particularity

: but it lasts ... for
ever and ever
I'm a boy on a swing,
winds reversing always
over the night-sky my carpet

Lover that I hope you are.... Do you need me?
For the vessel I am is like of a rare crystal
that must be full to will any giving. Only
such a choice at the same time is acceptance
as it is a demand high and arrogant.

Christ! I talk about love like a manoeuvre of
armoured knights with drums and banners!
Is it for you whose least whisper against my skin
can twang me like a guitar-string? for
myself? or for something stronger than the saw
that cuts diamonds, yet is only a thought of perfection?

And this is not a guarantee, only a promise
made by one who can't judge either his weakness
or his strength...but must throw them
like dice, one who never intended to play
for small stakes, and who once having made the greatest
        gamble
and lost, lives for the next total throw.

If this brain's over-tempered
consider that the fire was want
and the hammers were fists.
I've tasted my blood too much
to love what I was born to.

But my mother's look
was a field of brown oats, soft-bearded;
her voice rain and air rich with lilacs:
and I loved her too much to like
how she dragged her days like a sled over gravel.

Playmates? I remember where their skulls roll!
One died hungry, gnawing grey perch-planks;
one fell, and landed so hard he splashed;
and many and many
come up atom by atom
in the worm-casts of Europe.

My deep prayer a curse.
My deep prayer the promise that this won't be.
My deep prayer my cunning,
my love, my anger,
and often even my forgiveness
that this won't be and be.
I've tasted my blood too much
to abide what I was born to.

Part Two

1970–83

I'm a tough guy from Tough Guy Street.
The farther you go the tougher they get
And I live in the last house.

Anon., quoted by James T. Farrell
as a Chicago folk-saying, in *Studs Lonigan*.
(Actually it's Canuck.)

Down Great George Street, up to the station;
The skirl of the pipes the very thrill of your nerves
With the pipemaster (only man who has the Gaelic)
Ahead with his great baton, his strut and toss proud
    as any man who's ever walked.
This is where we came in; this has happened before
Only the last time there was cheering.
So few came back they changed the name of the regiment
So there're no cheers now. Tho there are crowds
Standing silent, eyes wide as dolls' eyes, but brighter
Trying to memorize every face

This is where we came in. It happened before.
    The last time was foolishness
Now's got to be done because of the last foolishness.
In the ranks, perfectly in step (with the pipes
    even I'm perfectly in step)
I'm thinking of *Through the Looking Glass*:
The White King's armies marching while he sleeps;
We are his dream.... At least it seems that way.
They're so clumsy the front line topples
The second line topples over it; and on it goes
    – line after line, eyes glazed straight forward
Shoulders back, spines held stiffly unnatural
Toppling over the line before

So few came back they abolished the regiment.
I was lucky – sickness and bad marksmanship.
Man by man we'd sworn to take our guns back,
    man by man we didn't.
One man – one war – that's all he's usually good for.
Now a strange short-haired subculture
Glares at us out of the TV set

Snarling the news, every phrase or disguised opinion
    as if it was a threat, which it is.
This is where we came in
It's happened before.
This last time was right
But ended in foolishness.
It has happened before, could happen again
Despite the fact that stuff is out of date.

Gentle Goddess! Bride of the wounded!
No flame searches so deep as your white tongue's caressing

No moment sets itself inside itself as yours does
Last thing that moves in the delicacy of day....

Gentle Goddess! Gentle Goddess!
                              JEN
                                    TIL
            GAW'
                                    DESS!
How is it I call her gentle whom I saw last night
Among the fires of a city's noisy dying?
Her eyes came out in the spaces between various-coloured
      plumes
Of smoke – plumes like the tails of giant felines waving over
      all....
They were like the moons of an alien planet;
And in each eye there was a wheel-shaped cage
In which little rodents ran or hesitated forever
Sometimes switching directions....

Gentle Goddess! Gentle Goddess!
                              JEN!
            TIL!
                                    GAW'!
            DESS!
Lady I wish I was by nature permitted
To wish I was religious; and if I was a sniper
To wish every bullet inscribed with a prayer
That he not be hit but frightened narrowly;
That he be, in some mind-corner aware
I was right, and the clipped irregular suddenly ending
Song of the bullet shock him into qualitative growth....

Or wish for a wound, incapacitating only briefly;
Or failing all else, wish for a soul to pray for . . . .

Grey-feathered soul, trembling like a bird in a cat's jaws:
No move of yours through the decorated kingdoms
Hasn't had its contradiction . . . .
                                        What I must wish
Is that in every turn I be honestly wrong or right,
That I question my honest civilization, my honest savagery,
And within the compass of certain honest necessities
I remain honest enough to change

Gentle Goddess! Bride of the wounded!
The wounded to death, to whom there's no time to say more;
And the wounded – the only wounded
Whether the wound be open or bacterial, of thoughtlessness
        or of the mind;
For all of these I hope to wish to pray
In your name, whether it be Birth or Death, Changelessness,
        Change or the changelessness of continuing change;
That friend and enemy know you, that
When consciousness is fluttering like a moth, the heart
        likewise

They know you: And breathe themselves out with their thanks

It's the last stormtime of winter. As if the ghosts of ancestors
Forgetting even they are ancestors
Were wandering. They cannot groan so the trees groan for
    them;
The hiss of the snows is their wordless breath.

Survivors they were who hunted survivors
The stumbling moose, the slumbering bear, the rabbit...
Always winter was the season of their wanderings
And now they wander like fragmented crystals of snow.

It's the last stormtime, when summer seems a fantasy,
Something dreamt of, a visit to another planet.
Gawd I feel I was an oversize dumptruck
Loaded with everything that fell this year;
All the snow, all the soot and debris in it.

Somewhere else, in both space and time,
The snow's cleaner, but no less fierce.
Now when even the dullest eye looks up for the faintest hint
    or hope of blue;
When it's unthinkable that winter once was pleasant;
Now's the thing like a moment when somewhere, somewhen
The ancestors are wandering; cold, hunger, tiredness,
The void in the head where there should be memory – all
    these are the same.

They must slay the great beast of spring
Whose decay is a field of berries, whose decay is the one-eyed
    sun
In whose yellow lashes all colours revive
And the living remember who they were
So the dead perhaps may remember too.

In speaking Ojibway you've got to watch the clouds
turning, twisting, raising their heads
to look at each other and you.
You've got to have their thoughts for them
and thoughts there'll be which would never
exist had there been no clouds.

Best speak in the woods beside a lake
getting in time with the watersounds.
Let vibrations of waves sing right through you
and always be alert for the next word
which will be yours but also the water's.

No beast or bird gives a call
which can't be translated into Ojibway.
Therefore be sure Ojibway lives.
There's no bending or breaking in the wind
no egg hatching, no seed springing
that isn't part of Ojibway.
Therefore be sure Ojibway lives.

The stars at night, their winking signals;
the dawn long coming; the first
thin cut of the sun at the horizon.
Words always steeped in memory
and hope that makes sure
by action that it's more than hope,
That's Ojibway, which you can speak in any language.

AT DAWSON CREEK HOTEL

Like single rocks from space hitting the moon
The fist of the Québécois in the next room
Thump...Thump...Thump...Far into the night – I make no
    objection
The turbulence of his mind matches the turbulence of mine.

In the daytime he has visitors. Thru the wall
I can't make out much except his larynx grating again and
    again
"C'est pa'd' juste... C'est pa'd' juste!"*

The town's afflicted with workless wanderers.
Indian and White... Native and foreign
They came in honesty, came with honour;
Came to labour: and there is none.

This town afflicts the workless wanderers
(*c'est pa'd' juste – c'est pa'd' juste*)
Too much to care for, to care for without purpose
(*c'est pa'd' juste – c'est pa'd' juste*)

Late into the night I hear his fist. Late into the day
I hear his voice as if it was grinding rock.
(*"C'est pa'd' juste... C'est pa'd' juste!"*)

---

* "This is not justice...."

Like a shawl thrown over a woman's shoulders
The narrow cloud trailed along the mountain
And there was me, shouting to Red Lane
"Get it Red! Get the ITNESS of it!"

I'd studied that mountain for three years
And studied many similar clouds
And nothing had impressed me so much
That the poem is not the thing;
So high and yet its contours so smooth
And clouds like that so appropriate to it.

I never knew a man so strangely himself
That thought of him was so much as he was
(perhaps I saw him, even then, as I see him now
    – the absoluteness of death
                  cast on a thin screen of life)
Perhaps I was begging him to write the poem I couldn't
The poem of the mountain which would be the mountain.

I never knew a man who so combined
Consent and refusal. In him they were one and the same.
The mountain's still there and Red's dead;
But what'll it be in ten million years' time?
The hills are dissolving like sugar candy,
The process slower, but no less certain.

What will Red Lane be then?
               Still part of the rocks
    – an undiscovered fossil.

The hawk swoops down upon three crows
But the crows have seen him;
Suddenly they become nimble
Their erraticness an advantage.

To the hawk's life, they'll give no tribute of death.
          They attack and
In half a minute it's over.
Knowing the slightest tremor of the wind
The hawk can climb faster.

Soon the crows have forgotten
Will tell no stories, sing no songs of triumph.
Neither does the hawk know humiliation;
Skimming, finding the updraughts
He distances further and further
Smaller and smaller in the heights.

Though he must find a victim or die
Urgency's no use to him.
He's not equipped to think of it.

England's a cretin's grunt dressed up in a crumbling gothic
Whose spires are spikes aimed at the curdling heaven,
Curdling, going rotten, and so close you can guess
Why its inhabitants once thought aiming their barbs that way
Required just a "tally-ho" and no mental effort.

England's a Lewis Carroll chessboard with all
      Shakespeare's characters
Overwhelmed in a sudden protracted deluge of applause,
      fossilized in their most sententious poses
With, crawling among the statuary, the English workers
Whining of how they're the slaves of Capital;
Contemptuous of anyone who's not a slave of Capital.

England's not the source of all our woes, just the source
      of the most annoying ones;
Where the aspiring-to-be-bright aspire to be gentlemen
Only to discover this is the contemporary age –
      there are no gentlemen.
Trained to administer colonies, they discover with surprise
There're so few colonies left the competition
Is so fierce it's like a river full of crocodiles –
      no other edible beast in sight:
So they come to Canada and other naïve places
To administer the colonies of the American Empire.

England is. England is. England is. If you want to put it
      into words
You've got to be drunk as Churchill was most of the time;
A place where every good resolve erodes in a gruel
      of bad oratory,
A rotten Stilton cheese mecca to expatriate Englishmen
      down to the sixth and tenth generations.
Who dare not proclaim their loyalty with their own flag

But invent the Red Ensign and similar bastard rags
Which on various chickenpox scars of Earth denote
    the inhabitants
Continuously held-back coughs of submission to a
    dead-and-gone-slavery.

Many's the time when I was on the job
The sawman came to me:
"You're able – and you can work fast.
Why don't you handle the big saw?"

Upon which I'd hold up my hands
Thumbs and fingers spread out:
"Look. Count 'em. Ten, isn't there?
That's how many there's going to be!"

Take a rain-trip. Neither swallow it or smoke it,
But stand out in the rain, in shorts a loin-cloth or naked
With every aperture of your body open
And your thoughts a bubble from horizon to horizon.

Think a while and the clouds will be giant spiders
With every raindrop, through all the time of its course
A leg... These are million-legged spiders
With every contradictory current of the air
Bending each one of the millions of legs
In hazardous curves – so they dance.

Get the cool of it... the chance taste
Of drops the open-bellied wind throws at you:
Eyes can taste then: the exits for sperm and urine
Can taste, and if the orifice for words
Opens for some statement which never issues
What comes in is a rain of tastes... each itself part
        of the statement.

And every gable, every eave can be forgotten. What there is
Is a division of the rain, each house-ridge an edge
From which the water slides two ways, thin enough maybe
To let the molecules be counted; a house is
A place under a shifting fabric of rain, veiled at the sides by
Droplets spilling as a new state of the rain-being
After many other states have been....

And the trees – forget them. See them as a staggering
Of the legs.... Drops change and fall in a different order
Not even themselves, other things of their own kind.
See the spaces where the trees might be

If you saw things differently
As saris of rain in a changed condition;
Ghosts of the rain which will continue to rain
When the rain is gone – its memory.

We carried him who'd often carried us
Like boats on his torrent, often by scorn
Which because he loved so much, could be borne
Up and down paths strung to precipices,
A milder man those days than he once was
For we'd tempered him with criticism,
Now I wish in those hills and fat chasms
Perversely for a burst of his foreign curses.

Then I was thinking aloud: "Comrade Bethune
Don't die on us! Half your skill
Hasn't been shown us yet... and it never will."
He jerked his head and cracked a cranky grin;
"What whining's this? Can it be Communism?
I've set one mark. Let's see some competition...."

I, MILTON ACORN

after Brecht

I, Milton Acorn, not at first aware
That was my name and what I knew was life,
Come from an Island to which I've often returned
Looking for peace, and usually found strife.

till I came to see it was no pocket
In a saint's pants while outside trouble reigned;
And after all my favourite mode
Of weather's been a hurricane.

The spattered colour of the time has marked me
So I'm a man of many appearances;
Have come many times to poetry
And come back to define what was meant.

Often I've been coupled, and often alone
No matter how I try I can't choose
Which it shall be. I've been
Ill-treated, but often marvellously well-used.

What's a man if not put to good use?
Nothing's happened I want to forget.
What's a day without a notable
Event between sunrise and sunset?

My present lover finds me gentle
So gentle I'll be in my boisterous way.
Another one was heard to call me noble.
That didn't stop her from going away.

To be born on an island's to be sure
You are native with a habitat.
Growing up on one's good training
For living in a country, on a planet.

Shall I tell you the soil's red
As a flag? Sand a pink flesh gleam
You could use to tone a precious stone?
All its colours are the colours of dreams.

Perhaps only the colours *I* dream
For I grew under that prismatic sky
Like a banner of many colours
Alternately splashed and washed clean.

The Island's small... Every opinion counts.
I'm accustomed to fighting for them.
Lord I thank Thee for the enemies
Who even in childhood tempered me.

I beg pardon, God, for the insult
Saying You lived and were responsible
... a tortuous all-odds-counting manner
Of thinking marks me an Islander.

Evil's been primary, good secondary
In the days I've been boy, youth and man.
I don't look to any rule of pure virtue
But certainly not continuance of this damned....

Damned! Damned did I say? This glorious age
When the ancient rule of classes is hit
And hit again. History's greatest change
Is happening... And I'm part of it.

IF YOU'RE STRONGHEARTED

after Auden

If you're stronghearted look at this Island;
red gouges of creeks at low tide and
the stronger red which spreads behind plows.
Don't hold your tongue too long, it'll swell
with so much good and so much bad to say.

If you're stronghearted look at the clouds
growing and raising heads to look themselves,
opening mouths to say what should be said.

If you're stronghearted ripple your way
up and down over low green-patched hills.
You can look from twenty feet and be unobserved
except for the fire of your eyes.
Strong eyes... they've seen such beauty
that a nerve runs from each to the heart.

If you're stronghearted put your ear to the ground
to hear the lilt and cut of soft voices
discussing enemy moves without fear.

"Well sirs, then we're agreed on the plan.
Black John here will fire on this Englishman
And miss (make sure of that, lad
The battle depends on this)
One quarter mile on, White John
Will miss too, but closer, and if that
Stinking piece of rent-collecting manure
Who dares call himself a gentleman
Keeps on, Red John will shoot his horse.
Old John here will then happen along
And lend him his horse – the red stallion.
Once he's on that beast, no more worries
Except to collect the remains, living or dead
And carry them back to Charlottetown
And, of course demand our expenses
Be very particularly
                    angry
                        about that."

THE FIGURE IN THE LANDSCAPE
MADE THE LANDSCAPE

The figure in the landscape made the landscape
Like the farmer you see in this painting I've imagined
Pre-Confederation, pre
Any moment you might wish to be in or not
Since the loyalists came, instantized themselves into rebels
Or when they were joined, reinforced by Scottish clansmen.

His beard may be like a sprucetree upside down
Or scraggy from recent Indian mixture;
But whatever his eyecolour was a moment before;
Preoccupied with work, keen with observation,
Wild in a laugh or soft and genial;
Now the man invisible in the picture
As the painter's invisible but still there;
The landlord's agent sees nothing but hellfire.

"Ye'll get no rent for woods ye didn't cut,
Stumps dug out with a horse I had to borrow,
Land I ploughed – me and my old lady
Who wasn't so old those days – me in harness
And her at the handles;

A road I made with friends and relatives;
And the wharf. When's there goin'ta be a wharf here?
Don't bother with that. We'll manage without ye
As well as we'll manage without payin' rent."

Except four things I'll mention later
Everything he wears or carries
Is his own – right from the sheep's back
It was made by him or his kin, even the dye
Whose base, if you want to know, spouted from his body.

Four things were bought or obtained otherwise
... his hat (tho he himself trapped the beaver
His boots tho it's himself grew slaughtered and skinned
        the beast, tanned the leather;
And the musket past which his hellfire eyes glare.

Of course he saw the agent coming
If not as usual warned long in advance. He's never worked
        long
Anytime in his life with his head always down.
Always straightened for thirty seconds every five minutes
To scan the landscape for any strange object,
And as a vacation for maybe five seconds
Bathing in its beauty like it was his own sweat.
Islanders to this day retain this habit.

And the landscape rolling like a quilt
By one of those strange fitnesses
Of geography and history
Is red and green, red and green, two rebellious colours;
Clearings and woodlots, clearings and woodlots:
Seldom even today is an entire farm cleared
As woodlots made the land difficult
To spy out, for anyone not familiar with the place,
And besides that make good ambuscades.

Today the tourists, pawns who don't know they're
Pawns in a new still-just-brooding
Struggle for the land, skim past
Or poke around slow wondering
At the beauty and gentleness
Of the Island countryside, the Island people
(those who fight best are kind to each other)
With every turn in the road a new surprise.
Few of them think that's the way it was designed.
"A lovely land," they say, "and peaceful"
When every part of it was laid out for war.

Not in battle but in dreams between
did fear jar us, for the sun
was round, gold, so much like a coin
it symbolized the monied rays
which never set on the empire we fought.

Two years with only Saint-Denis
to raise a shout for victory
while our muddled leaders waited
like stunned bulls for defeat at Saint-Eustache.
We who'd so often been victors
and often were to be victors again
tasted the bloody clay at Montgomery's:
fourteen battles of Kingston... all lost.
Give the grudging comment to ourselves... we were
        persistent.

Two years of rallies. Two years of rebuff,
our arms makeshift and unstandardized.
Scarcely one man's bullet would fit another's gun.
Quarrelling leaders, percolating spies
... on every field the enemy waited for us
armed and disciplined, well-informed and organized
... never cowards, whatever else they were.
Every fighting race has some such record
shuffled among the leaves of its history:
but this was for our freedom....

Never forget we are a fighting race
until the days of war are done.
Never forget Ortona, where we faced
the most bestial of an army of beasts.

It being beasts against men, we men won
and marched over their bodies, in the direction of Rome
(we seem to remember taking Rome, but no matter)
Stoney Creek, Lundy's Lane, Beaver Dam
: remember them; the world's greatest empire
to be was trying to be born
and we most obstinately delayed her
... keeping Ontario a spear in her side.
We stopped in the rain and stinking mud of Passchendaele
to get the puzzling news we'd won
though there was nothing we could see worth winning;
as none of this will have been worth doing
and those who died in it, truly dead
till we win what we lost in 1837.

When we tell this now it seems strange
to say the name "Canada" tragically,
giving her person and sex; to speak
of ancestors as "we". This
is a consequence of our defeat
to speak of our love for the land
or any love, remotely
as if the words didn't fit our lips;
to speak of history any more eloquently
than tersely – "not done yet"

When the squall comes running down the bay,
Its waves like hounds on slanting leashes of rain
Bugling their way . . . and you're in it;
If you want more experience at this game
Pull well and slant well. Your aim
Is another helping of life. You've got to win it.

When you're caught in an eight-foot boat – seaworthy
    though –
You've got to turn your back, for a man rows backwards
Taking direction from the sting of rain and spray.
How odd, when you think of it, that a man rows backwards!

How odd, when you think of it, that a man rows backwards.
What experience, deduction and sophistication
There had to be before men dared row backwards
Taking direction from where they'd been
With only quick-snatched glances at where they're going.

Each strongbacked wave bucks under you, alive
Young-muscled, wanting to toss you in orbit
While whitecaps snap like violin-strings
As if to end this scene with a sudden exit.

Fearfulness is a danger. So's fearlessness.
You've got to get that mood which balances you
As if you were a bird in the builder's hand;
For the boat was built in consideration
Not only of storms . . . of gales too.

Though you might cut the waves with your prow
It'll do no good if you head straight to sea.
You've got to make a nice calculation

Of where you're going, where you want to be,
What you need, and possibility;
Remembering how you've survived many things
To get into the habit of living.

That corrugated look to water
– grey with a glitter:
I've been told now that it's ice;
microscopic bergs clashing,
making music of many thin tones
too faint for us to hear.

Gulls fly labouring
low and straight, point to point;
bouncing off air pressed down
by their own wingbeats,
tips walking on
the same wingtips reflected.

No day this for men
to be at business on the water
– no longer ours, but winter's.
Wind's so raw you don't know if
you're freezing or boiling;

though there are no waves, only
winking, glittering
ripples flittering against
downthrusting cold chunks
of air. We glimpse
it from the land through chinks
between hills, trees, houses;
and eyes ache
with brief sightings of
light shooting
flying needle
-icicle rays.

The wind rustles the forest
like a many-fingered hand
stroking a cat's fur.

Many times I've trembled
to the trees' ecstasy,
mistaking for fear
the lust of that touch.

When you touch me I shiver
half-hopeful at fate still hidden,
as it took me years to learn
the tickled happiness of the forest.

I worry about the shape of my skull
Now that half my teeth have gone and gone.
If I'm ever taken by a head-hunter
Or dug up by a geologist
Will I be placed proudly on a shelf of honour
Labelled *Homo grossus superbus*,
Or whatever words correspond in head-hunter;
Or be grudgingly and briefly
Displayed, like a supercilious
Badge a hippy wears for a week;
Then to rest tormented in some dusty broom-closet?

I worry about those red and white
Citizens of my veins – the blood-cells;
Especially as I'm subject to nosebleeds ...
Every dripping drop condemning millions
To death in the parching air.
Should I carry in my pocket
A collection of marbles for monuments
Then to worry about them being kicked away?

I worry about there being no life on Mars
And about there being after all, perhaps
Some life on Mars. This uncertainty
To my dreams makes me worry
About my reveries offending against truth.
How many times will succeeding critics
Put a finger on a line of poetry
And nail me to a cross built of my own lies?

I worry about Terra Australis Incognita
– the great southern continent drawn on old maps.
How dare it not exist?
How dare a limit to the Earth's size

Exist? Friends, I worry
That I can't today go voyaging
Past the limits of limits, except at great expense
Into a space so vast
To measure it in miles or kilometres
Would keep me saying precisely one number
From birth till death and not be done.

I worry, curiously little
About my own fatality
But of the finality of billions of lives
Being most fatefully over.
But most of all I worry
About the shape of my skull, all those teeth gone!
How will it look being held up
By an executioner proclaiming:
"Here's the head which dared question
The complicated necessity of injustice;
And worst of all gave its own answers!"
Will he open the jaw to general laughter?
How will it look spiked to a sharp post
Beside the freeway as a warning
... leading a torchlight procession?

Younger Belle was lonely, but now
the men brandish forearms in her kitchen,
shake themselves out with laughter.
Wives, glad they're not at mischief
respect her jet-black mane from a distance

for she'll have no drinking, have no drinking
have no – well perhaps a little one:
but if the measure get more than "some"
it's "Here's your tea. Where do ye want it
down yer throat or over yer head?"

Edwin with his glasses, his pipe
and freckled spare-tipped fingers
she married at twenty-nine – had to
(everybody had to but
                              the joke is
she made Edwin sign a certificate
or signed one for him . . . the tales vary).

Edwin is an excellent carpenter
because, they say, he thinks like a board;
but his joy and vocation is moonshining
in which every bubble tells him what's doing.
Says four words in a day
and two of them are "No ma'am."

There's a contest of daughters for the affections
of the youngest, a son
born beside a mare munching clover.
She bore him alone
and he was most reluctant to breathe.
"Kill or cure!" Belle hissed through teeth
whose canines are long and sharp like a wolf's.
What a whack it was: and what a yell!

"Daddy" in our family means just one man;
Six generations ago, since two have followed me.
On other lines we trace our ancestry
Farther back, but "Daddy"
Seems to start with himself, like Adam.

Tho he might sometimes've wanted to hide
He never pushed a bush in front of his face.
Went clean-shaven when most men wore beards,
Perhaps because he was red-headed
And abhorred exaggeration; maybe because
He couldn't manage to grow much more than a fuzz.

He went to sea as a carpenter,
Became the master of his own schooner
And for a while owned a little fleet
All of which was lost in one storm;
Begged bought or borrowed another schooner
To sail safely the rest of his life.

When winter came and ice
Floated and ground, crashed back and forth across the Gulf
He'd sail his swift lateen to the Caribbean
Leaving supplies and one instruction
"NEVER TURN AN INDIAN FROM YOUR DOOR..."
Which Great-Grandmother interpreted
As he would've, getting down to situations
: - "Never turn ANYONE from your door..."
When Spring came our folks were always poor.

Describing wicked men is easy...
In good men you've got to look for a flaw; otherwise
It's painting a picture without shadows.
Daddy didn't drink, smoked sparely,

Didn't save his love, only his money;
Spoke with such a clear modulation
He could be heard from poopdeck to prow, masthead to wheel.

Only a hurricane could make him yell;
In short was perfect – except one thing:
At visiting time he'd sometimes climb the roof,
Use his cane to knock on the door
To say in a voice so polite it was sinister
"Would ye be the kind of man to let me in?"

My lips will not writhe,
Speaking of this old-time human,
Into the shape of a runic letter
Denoting an ancient secret, sacred wisdom.
His times were younger than ours, he
May have been a foundling
And furthermore, strange as he was,
Much as he did, he still died young.

He first fell ill in 1913
And learned – this man already thought so wise
His slightest murmur was listened to
Had a heart which also was murmuring.
"Nothing serious, just take it easy
And you'll live to be old. Something else'll kill you."
How could Daddy take it easy?
Life was hard for him, his lover and his children.
Could he go on? Of no help? A burden?

He went home and undressed
(small wiry body – muscles and all)
Took to bed, drank his last cup of tea, his first bottle of rum,
Commenting, "Just as I thought – not much."
Turned his face to the wall, wouldn't speak
Unless spoken to, seemed to be thinking
Of too many things with no time to be said.
In three weeks he was dead.

164

I wanted to love you, maybe forever
and you wanted to offend your God.
The pines had no voice but their perfume;
stars winked signals in no code I knew.
No one told me this blessing
in your ravelled mind was a deed of hate.

After'ds, puzzled and enraged, I wrote:
"Didn't you feel joy sweep us pure and
our hearts beat against each other swift
as two wings of a swallow?
Your sweat was sweet as berries.
How could your own body lie to you?"

Man of all fates he seemed to be
Though one fate held him fixedly.
It's not so much your fate as how you carry it;
Bravery being useless without wit
As wit's useless without bravery.

Both expressed in the very way he walked:
No more than a boy, no less either.
My name in greeting came out of him with such timbre
It seems in memory a part of his own;
And day or night the crown of his woolly scalp
Sought out whatever was the zenith star
To move from suspended by a cord of silver.

Harmless to the harmless, hurtful to the hurtful:
Once I was shown a splotch of blood on the ground
Clotting thick like a red map of Africa.
"Jim did that!" There was another name, that of the vessel
Which had held that blood. It's well forgotten.
You didn't have to especially watch your words
With him. He listened for the intent.

His mother was to all appearance white,
Surprising me; being a child I commented.
She laughed entirely, hair long and dark, skin of celtic
        fairness;
What was surprising by any standard
Was that she married such an old gnarled smallish man
With nothing to show his worth, except these evidences
Right to the edge of understanding, this woman and this son.

They and all their like left town
There being too few remaining

Some retained the name but not the colour.
When I returned years later Jim was gone
Leaving me thinking of a Moorish knight, lance raised
Either in threat or greeting, take it as you like.
If you find me strangely familiar
In my vehemence, to some measure
All I think and do is in memory of him.

JOE EUSTON

I've often known Joe Euston to bet on his eyes.
"Which one is glass?" he'd ask
as the tavern started to sway;
                                    and the beerfog
crept by amber pseudopods
out from under tables, oozed from corners.

No one else ever won. Because I swear
upon a stack of bibles, bubbles and typewriters;
whichever eye was bet on he'd take out the other
and there they'd sit . . . both laughing;
one from its proper socket and one from the table.

Bump, bump, bump little heart
along this journey
we've gone together,
you piping all the fuel.

You're fistsize, and fistlike
you clench and unclench,
clench and unclench
keeping this head upright
to batter its way
through the walls of the day.

There's a slash of burnt grass beside the 401
Where a tanker crashed and tumbled.
The driver, whom people ran to rescue
Yelled, "Get back . . . She's going to blow!"

Don't ask his name. I don't know.
Pick one yourself. It's happened more than once.
For writing poems like this
I'm pronounced a droll Canadian dunce

By American professors
Whose countrymen tax the truckers' sweat,
Am barred from universities
Lest I lead students out of error.

To record the acts of the truckers
Would crack the slats of hierarchy
Though anyone who often shares the road
With them, could add a story:

Not only the quick will
To flick a pass of life to you
But observation so skilled it checks
Bolts on a fast-revolving wheel.

If a trucker signals you over
Neighbourly compliance is best.
It may be to ask a favour
But more often do a kindness.

I'm a trucker of necessary dreams
Slapping roads and crosswinds, coast to coast.
Do justice to truckers and poets;
At fifty-two I've outlived most.

Quick calculation for that trucker
– chances of rescue? – chances of massacre?
Like one knowledgeable cell in one living body
He yelled, "Get back... She's going to blow!"

They did get back and she did blow
In a pyre dark-red as the planet Mars;
Monumental tongue which for a moment
Licked the sky clean of stars.

We talk, discussing the news.
The sun drives round us daily.
Did I say there's a slash of burnt grass?
Hell no. That was four years ago.

If a shard of steel unintentional
or worse, intentionally hurtled, should
sever me from an arm or leg
so I must do with metal or wood;

then'ld I, like a conscious tree
exhalt the glories of asymmetry,
wheel my body thru the new-found twists,
test the must-be-discovered flexibilities
of one ankle or one wrist.

If thru the perversity
of chance or aim, it shattered
my brain and left my body living;
from some darkness I'd eventually
struggle up; as even now I
hammer as on a door against
the mists of my stupidity.

What am I now, this instant, without
you? reader? lover? person in a crowd?
My poems are one long varitoned shout
to reach you and get an echo.
They are as well a listening
to land amidst your stir and hear you sing.

If my eyes should vanish, and night
come in like the clapping of two hands;
the sun shot down, the board wiped clean
of sun and sky leaving just their memory;
still part of the wind would be your voice
and part of the world would be your touch.

The orgasm doesn't end. This echo
is more than your voice. Wind pushes me
and I feel you nudging me again.
Here by the wrinkled sea, you three days gone,
your absence and return are both you.

Hair twitches on my arms. It always did.
I was myself before I ever met you;
but when you brought this gift, you
gave me as a gift to love
for you or anyone I'll still call You.

Because of you I've forgiven all my lovers
and if you betray me, I'll forgive you too.
My name in your voice, is in every birdcall.
I am the same, but even more so.

The orgasm doesn't end. This pulse
is the running of your tickling fingers.
Does it matter if I'm twenty or fifty?
I am the same, but even more so
in the ebb of the tide or its flow,
for you or anyone I'll still call You.

*Many Islanders fought World War II in the North Nova Scotia
Highlanders. There's this monument in New Glasgow, N.S.*

In a park by the river in New Glasgow
stands a kilted piper playing a dirge;
with all round the plinth of the monument
(so many in so small a town)
the names of the dead in the First World War.

This was put up by the citizens
and of course most of the names are Scotch;
survivors Scotch too for they calculated
            to a nicety in 1930
... how large a plinth for how many names.

Ten years after came another war
so behind they had to put up another stone
for names of the new born new dead; but
this time took precautions;
left a blank square yard and a half on the
            back of the stone.

But ... again but ... when you look round the stone
you find this is not a monument
        but an advertisement.
        for the names of two entities
        living in law
that of a monument company
and a firm of architects
are there (though the sculptor's name is absent.

In a park by the river in New Glasgow
stands a kilted piper playing a dirge

all in bronze, though not kept shone
                              :

all in silence
            Still you know it's a dirge
for the dead, some of whom could be husky today
: and for...
                  some of them hoped...
What exactly did they fight for?
        Yanks?
        to claim their victory?
        as if it was over themselves?
        their nation prisoner?
May the poem not end here;
                              the last note
not be a dirge....

POEM SCRAWLED ON THE RUINED WALLS
OF A FALL-OUT SHELTER

They've built an atomic age people cooker
on a campus ponderous with Western thought.
No defence . . . just a concrete womb-in-reverse
to crawl into and shrivel to nothing;
for deep-dark-deep in their guts they know that
for the fantastic wind from their yaps,
their folkgame of mishaps contrived for each other,
the only defence is Death.

My half-lame lover with your sweet nerve of life:
has a vital letter been burned? A job refused?
Some fumble-brained vampire stuck a tube in your heart
to siphon away joy he had no use for?
Don't let it wither you . . . . It isn't personal!
If they've ripped the clothes and hide off you,
put you – bare as those folk in anatomy charts,
under cold high pressure hoses . . . Don't feel rejected:
That's just society's hail and howd'yedo!

It isn't personal . . . . They intend no malice!
Your fresh air's peppered with cancer!
But they intend no malice!
The milk in your breasts is poisoned!
But they intend no malice!
The whole damn Pacific Ocean's poisoned, and your gonads
hold ten thousand generations of abortion!
But that's just life's old give and take, man, cool it
whilst they singe off the world like a dumb dead turkey!

They've built an atomic age people cooker
to symbolize the death before dying,
grey whisper of life, less than the dream of plants,
troubled stirring, vague hurt of hopes,

curses mumbled between sleep and sleep,
they've always tried to make
the long blue-lipped sigh of human existence.

When the survivors, if any, crawl out
on a world clinkered with skulls and fingerbones,
then'll be the time for their damn square virtues!
When wombs spew forth their monsters
with stings for pricks and toothed vaginas,
think of how they'll regulate sex!
with cow's milk radioactive Javex,
think of their austerity programs!
When brains grow on the outside of heads and
any maladjusted mechanic can blow up a country,
how they'll supervise thoughts! How earnest they'll be!
Can't you see them now facing facts?
Keeping a stiff upper lip? Adjusting to the group?
Can't you see them marching tried and true thru history,
stiff and straight as God Save The Queen,
till the whole promising world dies
from congestion of blood in the cerebellum?

My lovers . . . the moments are fingers of God
or Satan who is God's brother;
fingernails long as a teasing virgin's
like switchblades waving at your breastbone.

Instant by instant we're choosing life or the bugs of darkness,
the end of mankind as Man; and our only defence is life.

When Les Habitants glide onto the ice
A great bird out of time unruffles wings.
Every throat there is possessed by a spirit
So greetings arise from an angelic chorus.
Less a team itself than a living spirit
I'm told and want to believe
That, on a sheet of clear ice, each man
Can skate his name, cleanly as by hand.
Dashes represent the years when they don't own the cup.

I've seen with these two eyes, one second fractioned
By three cracking passes – the fourth shot a goal.
What would you call this but a miracle?
Popular thunder swells impatient.
The lions have arrived! Where are the Christians?

BY STILL MORE STUBBORN STARS

for Kenneth Leslie

There are men who can see one star break
Momentarily through a rake of clouds;
Guess which it is and thereupon stake
Course, life and many more thumping loud
Human pulses on a line more tenuous,
Through an incoherent stagger of shocks,
Than one by which a new spider launches
His wee red splot of life over world-tops.
By still more stubborn stars, against still more
Dreadful collisions, meaner misdirections
(loud and willing liars calling the score)
Do I make aim to steer this lusty pen
So finely shaped like spear or phallus
To save or kill as right as it fertilizes.

INVOCATION

You loved one, hurt one, loving one still strong...
If you were only an impossible vision
Why would you lurk – a quiet worm in my tongue
Wait and live to raise this invocation?
What did you look through, in Spook Canyon
Besides that smiling mask, carved from a tree –
Tools learning as they cut a growing wisdom
To top and ornament your poor wronged body?
You have entered me, dead but not done.

I've loved, and love the Earth. If you are Death
Stay around to summon more performance.
Is that smile kinder yet? Plumbing consent?
Wait for the laughter! It'll blow breath
Tumbling all your atoms to collect 'em
Till lungs pump, your heart flutters, eyes go wide
And I'll be wise, at last, to find a bride.
My vehicle accelerates, bright one. Come.

What I know of God is this:
That He has hands, for He touches me.
I can testify to nothing else;
Living among many unseen beings
Like the whippoorwill I'm constantly hearing
But was pointed out to me just once.

Last of our hopes when all hope's past
God, never let me call on Thee
Distracting myself from a last chance
Which goes just as quick as it comes;
And I have doubts of Your omnipotence.
All I ask is... Keep on existing
Keeping Your hands. Continue to touch me.

It's late October and the sap's retreating
From blanching twigs, limbs and trunks
Down past the frostline to set roots drunk
With power necessary for growth underneath
Cold's gelid breathlessness and pounding breath
Unseething quiet ice and whispering snow.
Shifting below, breaking new ground to sheath
New roots; the trees, I theorize, move slow to Spring
As we humans grow, or lose our youth.
The birds and bosses are flying south;
Some to play and some to hatch a second brood...
Some to plot the devil knows what cheating.

Whatever's good in us will be tested
While our hearts take the place of the sun:
For ours is not the kingdom. Ours is the power
In these cursed and cursing months, weeks and hours,
To direct the winter storms in our heads.
So one day, when they come back, tanned with will and wit
To seize April... We'll have taken it.

Oh Canada our home and chosen land
Such awe and reverence do those Yanks command!
Champions of liberty of their own brand...
Their liberty to take us all in hand.
Proudly we mock the United Nations now
That not every vote goes the American way;
We masters of the Canadian bow
Backs turned and arse up to the U.S.A.

Oh Canada beneath those shining skies
A Yankee deproduction line runs south.
If we don't stop it – it won't be stopped.
What curses will our sons and daughters mouth
When cheated before they drew a breath, they stare
At Canada, the cruel north stripped stark bare?

Joseph, you're mistaken. It's not me
Who's the god of your mumbling, muttering
Curses at mixed-up totality. You only see
A humbly proud, proudly humble . . .

                                    Only?

Did I say *only?* What sort of stuttering
Foul fluttering, gutter-plucked puttering
Word was that? Don't you call me *only!*

I'm a man. Whether calm or furious
These curious sounds I make are human words –
Though some say "human" to mean "less than human."
If you're worried by what I've said and done
To bother, itch and nag you with optimism;
Don't try to put me down. Haul down the Sun . . . .

Face brooding, changing like a clouded sky
Dark with grim thought, and with lips
Perpetually twisting for a word
That can't get out – so stubborn the jaw grips
His coiled brain's exit. There's drama
In this shaggy, blackbearded bum. I've wondered
What he's up to, thinks he's up to, would be up to
When he makes crude drawings alongside cruder verse.

What can I say?
     He should be more than he
Is, his dreams roll more. Red flame ought to
Run from his nostrils, smoke curl up from his eyes
And when he speaks it shouldn't be idiocy
Such as might be piped by a passed pawn
Whose master weighs sacrifice.
       Somewhere a lion yawns.

Weep for Tyre and curse that son-of-a-god
Who in fair fight was shoved off its wall;
Avenged that fright with fire and rancour.
Don't push the Gods. They have no sense of humour.

Tyre whose glory was its industry
Done by no slaves – free proletarians.
No noble arts, no Gods, no language but Hebrew
Borrowed from spectacular hillmen
Turned its merchants from profits pursued as far as America.

Until Alexander, called the Great
By Himself in his own time –
That fool gone mad on a lucky streak knocked on its gate;
Saying, "Greetings! I've been granted all.... All!
By my dear old Dad, who's a God
As, so to speak, it is a fact I am myself.
Submit to me and I'll direct fate
Into proper channels aided of course
By your astutely merited wealth."

Mechanics smeared with dye began to laugh
Raising mutters among the businessmen;
"We've surrendered and served kings but a –
Gosh if we yielded we'd be odd as Him."

When my look leaked out
thru the moisture of youth,
afraid they'd discover
it was really me,

I threw out a confusion of words,
handy labels to the confusion
of flesh about my rosy thoughts,
and gathered notions

like clues to guide detectives past me
to a stone-faced idol
on whom I'd carved my name . . .
but for men with whimsical eyes
those tricks don't work.

Now I cast out words like
hooks anyone may use
to fish my weltering insides
out, and help my fishing;

but the shuddering thing is
that people used to squint thru
my ruses and see me, but

today nobody can . . . as if
I'd hidden galaxies, thinking them ornamental buttons,
or the search invents
and reinvents me.

Arguing the craft so long unlearned
At Roblin Lake, Ameliasburg, me and my pal
Purdy fought; leaving no stone unthrown:
About internal rhyme, off-rhymes and thought-rhymes
Plus other quirks that work sometimes, hard-earned or
    suddenly known.

"Face it," I said to him, "you're a worker."
"Face it," he'd say to me, "you're petit-bourgeois."
At which I hit and splashed the roof, detecting Trotskyism;
And he splotched the stain of his brain on mine, detecting
    Stalinism:
Convincing, unconvincing each so well
We actually exchanged roles for some while.
One thing I came to think and still count so
Russian steel production
              at Roblin Lake
                    is zero.

My soul's no white wind-balanced gull.
It's a wolverine
... a bounce-and-hobble poke-and-punch
hunchback dangerous snuffling thing
whose salvation's the taste of the moment.

I'm the wobbly deep-eyed fawn, its prey
harried forever back into childhood
away from certainties
the eyes know and find
to cancel the tossy-clouded sky
and all such irrelevancies.

What a hot thirst it has!
For blood, the blood of battle
Where the flesh endures its sorrows
For its high joys and agonies!

Rankle-hearted jay, why are you scolding
Me working in my own field?
Perhaps you think the land's not mine?
Maybe she isn't, it's been in the family
For generations I'd count if I took the time;
On some occasions been well peopled
With other sweaty men, mostly neighbours
And just now much of this machinery
Isn't mine. It's borrowed. Or will be lent
Since we must take care of each other
Whilst counting every dollar made or spent.

Curse his soul! Here comes the sheriff
With all his threats remarkably similar
To ones such another made to my great-great-grandfather ....

Brown as an Egyptian, with eyes a pale shock
Six feet tall and straight, ninety hard kilos
Oedipus sets off on the road to Thebes
Not knowing that there is a Thebes.
Man must wander till he finds his place.

Simultaneously the Sphinx raises
Her turbulent eyes and nose sniffing –
Groaning with reluctance moves
Toward exactly what she doesn't know.
One must seek fate or else no fate's worthwhile.
Don't tell me life's a gamble. Death waits.

A line of wild canaries from a wire
Leaped at once in mutual startlement,
Cruciform wings flung out for quick beats
When I gave them a fox's look of desire
I think, when I was about seven;
Living and wanting metabolic fire.

My bluebird seen about then wasn't neat
Dead in the middle of a dusty track.
I'd seen them aloft in the living act
Of flight, but it has been a long retreat.

"Golden Orioles," I was corrected.
Another woman called them yellow flickers
As photons dance yet in my eyelashes
From the yellow sun of that season
When they came on high winds, left on new ones.
"Flying Dandelions," was my opinion.

Could I forget an arm, a leg, an eye
Which I had once and then had amputated?
If I could do that thing...then sure I'd
Deny how dialectically mated
We were...one of us the bird and one the air
But which one which? Two tunes in one song
...but who the melody, and who in there
To swing wrong when one was right, right when one was
      wrong?

Maybe that's an incorrect putting of it
And I say this only for argument:
My loved crossed and lost one...we fit
So well in our joint seizures, wild entanglements
Our juices must have splattered over planets
Fertilizing alien forget-me-nots.

In a storm the dull gulls flock inland.
The tern, the gallant tern makes out to sea;
Tacking, slanting against a forty-knot wind
To where the action is, and plumb shifts
Like hands of a clock with springs gone wild;
Fishing at their best where nothing stays pinned;
Swirling in flocks like snow upon green drifts:
Like a mind never at rest, they are at rest.

Realisant souls are the souls solidly
Set in these unsolid worlds and spaces.
With everything restless, nothing staying just so;
I keep in this eternal state of fission:
Back from a mission, off towards a mission;
Simultaneously I return and go.

No music from the bar. Damn Sunday
When no stripper wags her miscellaneous cuts
Of long pig, grotesquely meaning to look horny;
No singer whines impressions of a Yank in rut
Dripping polluted tears for damn dead Dixie:
Or Continentalist band beats and blares
You deaf, for what's meant to be eternity.

Idiotic noise, transmogrified to music
Or something like that, in my muffled room upstairs
Blurred me till I slept like a mosquito
Insentient to the worse civic bedlam –
Not quite serene: But now, fixed to this bed of fright
Through churning Sunday night in the volcano
Of a cannonading city; I'm frigged –
With no note to play against metallic discord
Short of getting up and making rage my lord...
Sleepless in Toronto – home of the homesick.

A most unghostly whistle, like a toy
Factory's – at the dim brown hour of four
Angled down from those ponderously stirred
Trees near the heaving, hunching slowpoke waves;
Used to shake me quick from dreams to wonder:
Till I knew it had to be a raven
Waking his relatives to plunder
Breakfast in this first, best, worst hour of war.

Now it's all routine, I'm up and to work
At a craft not the canniest raven knows
With half an ear for panic in the forest
Where they as well raise hell and drive blows.
Such quirks in my beloved reality:
The cruelest time for raven-work's best for me.

for F.R. Scott

Moon, queen of the tides and blood and me:
You're full tonight and I feel chunks of fury
Rattling about like meteors in my brainpan.
Which is prophecy, which vision memory
I hardly know or want to define.
If the past is dead, the future's buried with it.
This fist rising now will never slam down;
The moon never set... no more work for poets.

Last night I asked you to read me a bold
Scribble of yours, long part of my strength.
You said, "That poem's forty years old!"
Listen, old son, if it ever had significance
It has that now, and will have for ages.
The higher comes the moon, higher my thoughts rage.

MY BIG HEART

after Hikmet

Doctor listened with his stethoscope
To my inner machinery, and said
"You've got a big heart; thumping out time
All around your chest."

                          I said, "Yes I know
Since every undeservedly aimed blow
Ever driven at anyone has hit it.

"It's swelling all the time with hope
For this one, that one, others popping out
From wombs firing like machine-guns;
Each new person jumped and mugged for profit,
Learning language by hearing himself cursed
For being here and ever having done
Anything except for a bully's gain:
Starting with the crime of birth.

"Doctor: It's for a bomb I need this big heart
To smash those liars into a great squashed stain
When the pressure jumps too much, and it blows apart."

The thorn which guards the rose is much the same
As the teeth of the donkey wanting some
Living salad, blossoming, perfumed.
That admirable beast craves beauty
But the vicious little thorn rebuffs his love.

Small-nation patriotism, fighting the shove
Of a rich country after more booty;
Appears to be and is a similar game.
The resemblances are striking
As champion and challenger both use fists.
That's the way the world is.... I didn't make it.

Ancient worm tracks on a thin slab of shale
Over which beneficent ferns etch shadows
In sunlight on and off in a half gale
Reminded me of how alive my hand goes
As wee wriggle-beings moved across the mud
With a germinal urge to destination.

This ancestor of my fingers and fun
Has marked one spot for a very long time
Without a thought of assonance, syntax,
Cadence or message, breath-stop or end-rhyme.
"May the marks I make have such an impact!"
I wished with an elemental heart-thump.
At that age may this joker deal a trump!

Do I love you? Are you beautiful?
Don't I prove it every second night
Allowing for difficulties like menstruation
And drunkenness – that I love you well?
Please stop asking such difficult questions.
In times between, forgetting the sexual –
But not for long, don't I give demonstrations?

Oh God, I love you and do swear by love.
It's your soul I love, not exempting your body;
But I could hate you if you were beautiful:
Love you cursing from a twisted grin;
Love you if you were ugly as sin.
That's all I'm telling you. Don't crowd me!

I've a wonder to tell you
of Joe and my noise-ridden, pet-ridden, pest-ridden
brain folded like a complicated vegetable
around hate's push-button
that many a blind blackguard's finger
has pressed without intention;

but not Joe's. A subtle sinner envies virtue
with a love, a knowledge searing deep like acid;
and my image with all tendrils moving
a brown root moving
through soil, moves
through his eyes' mysterious black quarries.

A saint at his sins, a rogue practising good deeds
with supple fingers on the black and white keys,
can't be told apart. Maybe one shuffle
of a pack with good or bad luck sleightedly pricked in
from each touched card
changes the sides, the souls, the lines on men's faces.

I've a wonder to ask myself
of strength humming to each breath,
this extra heart throbbing my guts,
voice in my inner ear more real now
since Joe looked in, saw and listened;
for a man's spirit is given
and to recognize the spirit is to give it again
. . . a stronger dose.

Thoughts of good and evil are sharpedged
twisting in the wounds of saint and subtle sinner.

Each one's terrible in pain as a bull against the relentless
      matador;
but no kindness is lost,
no crime forgiven its victim,
this innocent world.

Those guys with wart-hard faces
gouged like an old field,
never took a holiday
on the date revealed
by red figures on the calendar
timidly appealed for
by the sometimes fierce legislature.

Mind you they weren't scared!
When the boss (an old hand himself
wistful for a day to spend
with a pipe, a pint of rum, and argument
asked round, they told him
if he cared
to grin away a day they'd
manage without him –
meanwhile they talked so much
of wives, relatives and broods,
I felt shrivelled by their virtues.

So I heaved and hammered
beside them all spring;
but when the yellow sun-glint
skipped the waves of summer,
began to see absences.
Each with a good excuse:
"The calves are loose
in the swamp – my well's dry,
we've got to witch for water"
. . . jobs alike in this way:
they took all day.

But with the autumn clouds tall
mirrored on their eyeballs,
the sky trailed like smoke with migrants,
they said, "We're after ducks
tomorrow. If that ain't liked
this job'll be over.
What the hell's life for?"
Those country guys lazed
at the right times, namely
when they damn pleased.

Hungry children have meek eyes.
They don't always cry, somehow
they know they're being punished.
They don't often speak aloud;
only their eyes say:
"Forgive me . . . Feed me!"

I confess to negative thoughts
. . . wantonly, wilfully, fascinated by ugliness,
seeing what a normal socially adjusted person
'ld ignore, and smirk to prove himself happy.
I've a morbid interest in life . . . . Why today
I watched delighted while a four-year-old boy grew
scar-tissue for his heart and mind's eye, learning
not always to love, always trust, always demand;
finding about *objects* – gas furnaces,
springboards, people, junk generally,
to fear, use, or bounce on, and never mind bruises.
He cried a little, then
began his own game of cowboys and handcuffs.

In Africa the sky's one big heat-blue eyeball,
seeming blind but with one hidden pupil
 – a vulture, easy-winged on invisible draughts.
Those birds have parcelled half the continent
into beats they patrol with cold-fire eyes staring,
staring, seeing everything that's done, noticing
everything that suits their practical purpose.
Let an animal lie down in awkward shape
and his appointed guardian angel swoops lower; the
next one sees him dip and edges in,
also swooping lower, and the next, and
if the creature's really in distress
the air fills with gauche cries, black pestiferous wings.

In Africa the other day a cop on *his* beat
saw a black man stand as a babe stands tottering,
reaching with a strangely discovered joy
to the kind wisdom in the sun's face.
It was a serious grief made him stand yet he laughed for the
      joy of standing;
and after him another stood ... ten thousand others
in all their tropical colours
stood laughing, danced and sang – even their curses were
      good-humoured:
but more efficient than vultures the white men gathered
with clubs, machine-guns, sabre jets,
and shouts of how unselfish they were.
The real forgivable vulture presiding in that smoking rag of sky
dipped hopefully, doubtfully;
but white ambulances came, and white doctors
who used the wounded tenderly, and the corpses.
Afterwards it was Sunday and they held a church parade
with hymns and a minister to tell
that tho a man, day by day and deed by deed, chooses the
      vulture's halfway death,
still by his grief,
by his desiring heart alone, not his deciding head,
he can choose a God who chooses life for him.

Beware of negative thoughts ... Lumumba's been arrested!
Be careful ... they want you too!
A white skin and a silly mouth
combined might save you for a while
but they've got measuring tapes, calipers,
black books for names.
They want everyone who isn't cut to a specific pattern,
and nobody is – not even themselves.

Like six hundred embryos at advanced terms
The crew of the Belgrano has been drowned
By means of the latest technology.
Glug-glug-glug! God save the Queen
In a chilly part of the Atlantic
Not to liberate the Argentines
Or Irish, or the Poles, simply for oil
Which you can get by planting olives.

The planet's second commonest liquid,
So cheap they must devise monopolies
In order to engineer a profit;
As profit's counted in this century...
Draw a breath if not too wet. God save the Queen
While propaganda swings the dimming beam.

(May 5, 1982)

IN MEMORY OF JOE EN-LAI

1898–1976

Never close the door on a parting friend.
Most inauspicious – that: hinting an end.
Watch him clear as he goes down the lane;
Photons from your eyes like a rain
Of blessings and good wishes. Hum
And memorize a song in his name
Which you'll hold secret till he comes again.

Never give a sign it's over and done.
Greet every new friend partly for his sake;
Thinking of him as just now gone and due back soon;
And if he doesn't return let loose that tune
To find and call him back wherever he's run.
Remember him behind in time, dream of him ahead.
Follow these instructions – even if he's dead.

NOTE: *The Chinese 'chou' is pronounced 'joe'.*

FOR MAO AND OTHERS

The old guy gets older... Accent more pronounced;
Sometimes only friends can understand him.
Is it senility or is it wisdom?
Quoting old, hard-learned, but also new axioms
He still moves easy with the Earth's spin
Recognized, taken into account.
Some say he's getting crazy like a fox –
Shouts at the morning as if he'd just been born.

"How are things today?" he asks; not "How are you?"
"What time is it?" "What's the date?" "What year?"
Then with a glint of pride and note of warning
"Have you justified your existence yet, this morning?" *
He won't be balked, waits with a nagging ear.
His second highest praise: "Me son; that's real sincere...."

*The folk-wisdom of the Maritime working people is just too profound for
academicians to really record. It shocks them silly. The line quoted is actually
a Maritime folk-saying.

Quetzecoatl: Big befeathered worm
Trapped between emptiness and atmosphere –
Void he can't breathe, air whose flavour
He can't stand – it's not quite right – squirms
From horizon to horizon, all night
While stars like needles impudently pierce him.

What a God! And what a coat he's got!
What shall I tell, and will I tell who what?
His feathers live as he does, swarm
Curling and uncurling, knotting and unknotting
Over that mightily bright, non-dazzling form.
Heard like modulated small winds in a pine-thicket
Within my lusting-to-comprehend head,
For no air-sound brooms it this far down
A whole gang of fiddlers is jazzing
Tunes like stroking fine cloth on fur.

Come ye faithful . . . Come ye faithless ones
To see this poet writhing, glad and half-crazy
Overseas, overland, overhead skyline to skyline . . . .

Dig up my heart from under Wounded Knee
Where it's been living as a root in the ground
Whispering the beat, to fool mine-detectors.
Though there may not be much Indian in me
That fraction was here first. It's senior.
Take this heart to grow a man around.

I shall be Heartman – all heartmuscle!
Strong and of longest endurance
I've acted, thought and dreamt to nurse my will
Proud for the day of the People's Judgement
When vision rides again and all that's meant
Is said and flashed from eyes once thought blind.
Fewer and fewer of us, rest now in silence.

INDEX OF TITLES

A NOTE ON THE TEXT

This selection was made by Al Purdy.

As indicated in the subtitle these poems were composed between 1952–83. The poems in Part One are drawn from *I've Tasted My Blood* (Ryerson Press, 1969), Milton Acorn's previous Selected.

The poems in Part Two appeared in *More Poems for People* (NC Press, 1972; revised edition, 1973); *The Island Means Minago* (NC Press, 1975); *Jackpine Sonnets* (Steel Rail, 1977); or are previously unpublished.

The series The Modern Canadian Poets *presents the finest poetry of contemporary English Canada. Each volume is drawn from the work of a single writer, either at mid-career or after a lifetime's achievement. General editor for the series is Dennis Lee.*

PUBLISHED TO DATE